An Essay on the Early History of the Law Merchant

being the Yorke Prize Essay for the year 1903

by

W. MITCHELL, B.A.

St Catharine's College,
Assistant Master at the Perse School, Cambridge

THE LAWBOOK EXCHANGE, LTD.
Clark, New Jersey

ISBN-13: 9781584776338

Lawbook Exchange edition 2006, 2010

The quality of this reprint is equivalent to the quality of the original work.

THE LAWBOOK EXCHANGE, LTD.

33 Terminal Avenue
Clark, New Jersey 07066-1321

*Please see our website for a selection of our other publications
and fine facsimile reprints of classic works of legal history:*
www.lawbookexchange.com

Library of Congress Cataloging-in-Publication Data

Mitchell, W. (William), d. 1912.
  An essay on the early history of the law merchant : being
the Yorke Prize essay for the year 1903 / William Mitchell.
    p. cm.
  Originally published: Cambridge : University press, 1904.
  Includes bibliographical references and index.
  ISBN 1-58477-633-1 (alk. paper)
  1. Law merchant--History. 2. Commercial law--History. I.
Title.
K1006.M58 2005
346.07'09--dc22   2005014285

Printed in the United States of America on acid-free paper

An Essay on the Early History of the Law Merchant

being the Yorke Prize Essay for the year 1903

by

W. MITCHELL, B.A.

St Catharine's College,
Assistant Master at the Perse School, Cambridge

Cambridge :
at the University Press
1904

𝔒𝔞𝔪𝔟𝔯𝔦𝔡𝔤𝔢:

PRINTED BY J. AND C. F. CLAY,

AT THE UNIVERSITY PRESS.

PREFACE.

THIS Essay does not in any way claim to be a Treatise on the subject. Lack of leisure has compelled me to omit many important topics and to deal all too briefly with others. My debt to previous writers—to Bensa, Huvelin, Schaube, Pollock and Maitland, and above all to Goldschmidt—is evident on every page ; as far as time and opportunities allowed I have gone to the original authorities. While the Essay was in the Press, I learnt that there were numerous fair rolls preserved in the Record Office and upon these I am at work. To Sir F. Pollock for kind suggestions I wish to express my thanks.

CONTENTS

CHAPTER I.

GENERAL CHARACTERISTICS.

THE Law Merchant has been aptly called "the private international law of the Middle Ages." It was regarded as a kind of jus gentium known to all the merchants throughout Christendom and the later writers who treated the subject laid stress upon its international character[1]. "The Law Merchant," wrote Sir John Davies in the 17th century, "as it is part of the law of nature and nations is one and the same in all the countries in the world; there is not one law in England, another in France, another in Germany, but the same rules of reason and the like proceedings are observed in every nation." This statement is too sweeping. Strictly construed it was not correct for the law as it existed in the 17th

---

[1] Malynes, *Lex Mercatoria*, 3. "The said customary law of merchants hath a peculiar prerogative above all other customs, for that the same is observed in all places."

Davies, *The Question concerning Impositions*, 10. "That commonwealth of merchants hath always had a peculiar and proper law to rule and govern it; this law is called the Law Merchant whereof the law of all nations do take special knowledge."

century, and it was still less correct for the Law
Merchant in the earlier stages of its evolution.
There was during the early middle ages no strictly
uniform system of mercantile law administered
throughout the whole of Western Europe either
in town or seaport or fair. The Great Fairs of
Champagne had their own style, usage and customs
which were at times altered in important points by
royal ordinance. The Merchants of Antwerp refused[1]
to submit to the law of London, and in the numerous
" lettres de foires " that have recently been discovered
at Ypres[2] the alien creditor has always to promise
not to recover his debt by any other law than the
law of Ypres. In Italy the special codes of commerce
that almost every great city possessed, show greater
or smaller discrepancies in almost every section, and
as a natural result, in several cities[3], the commercial

[1] *Monumenta Gildhallae*, vol. II. part i. 63. "Et cil de
Anwers ne passeront le pount de Loundres, si il ne voillent estre
desmenez par la ley de Loundres."

[2] Des Marez, *La Lettre de foire à Ypres*, p. 97 and
document 27. "Et li avant di Jehans de Flaringhes, borgois de
St Quentin, a encovent et promis par foit ke il ceste dette ne
requerra a nule loi fors a la loi de la ville d'Ypre."

[3] Statutes of Como, *Monumenta Historiae Patriae*, vol. XVI.
col. 28, cap. xxxi. A.D. 1281. "Quod ipsi consules possint cognoscere de omnibus quaestionibus negociatorum forensium et de
negociacionibus...quamcunque quantitatem ascendant et hoc tam
in cognoscendo quam in diffiniendo et execucioni mandando||
eisdem mercatoribus talem faciant et facere possint racionem et
non aliter, qualiter fieret mercatoribus Cumanis||in terra illius
mercatoris tunc querentis sub eisdem consulibus."

A.D. 1352. Spalati St. Nova, cap. xxvii. p. 246 (in *Monumenta Historico-Juridica Slavorum Meridionalium*). "Ordinatum
est quod amodo illud jus et justicia quod et que fiet civibus...

judges were ordered to give aliens no better law than their own citizens would have in the alien state.

Sometimes the variations in the Law were of far-reaching importance, and perhaps no better example can be given than the rules regulating the effect of Earnest money. Here, if anywhere, a definite and universal rule might be expected, for otherwise no merchant could be sure of his bargain. In the 13th century, however, the effect of the Earnest had not been finally settled. As a general rule it may be said that the payment of a God's penny was effectual - to bind a mercantile bargain, and Fleta expressly declares that such was the law amongst merchants. Edward I., for instance, gave the Earnest a binding force, as a favour to the foreign merchants. "Every contract," ran a clause in the Carta Mercatoria, - "between the said merchants and any persons whencesoever they may come, touching any kind of merchandise, shall be firm and stable, so that neither of the said merchants shall be able to retract or resile from the said contract when once the God's penny shall have been given and received[1]." At Avignon[1] the same rule prevailed; but there were exceptions. The Preston custumal[2] allowed the

Spalati in quacunque curia et foro cujuscunque civitatis...illud simile jus et justicia per similem modum et formam fiat in curia et foro civitatis illis hominibus."

1429. St. Merc. Brixiae, cap. 43. "Etiam possunt [consules mercatorum] forensibus tale jus reddere quale et quem ad modum in eorum terris redditur nostratibus."

[1] Maitland, *Select Pleas in Manorial Courts*, 133.

[2] Custumal of Preston, Article 12. Bateson, *Eng. Hist. Review* (1900), p. 497. "Item si Burgensis aliquid forum vel

seller to break the contract by repaying double the
Earnest, and the buyer by forfeiting five shillings.
In Italy most of the commercial statutes[1] declare
that if once an Earnest is accepted the contract is
binding, but Varese[2] again offers an exception to the
general rule, while in Sicily[3] it was the custom among
merchants to consider the Earnest merely as a

aliquem mercem emerit et hernas dederit et ille qui vendiderit de
foro suo penitebit duplicabit hernas ementis. Si autem emens
forum suum palpabit vel habebit forum vel quinque solidos de
vendente."

[1] Circa 1200. St. Antiqua Mercatorum Placentiae, cap. 65,
p. 20. "Et si quis de nusii (=mercantiae) jurisdictione mercatum fecerit...et...denarium dei dederit vel dari fecerit, illud
mercatum inter partes ratum haberi faciam."

1214, confirmed in 1265. St. Legis civitatis et insulae Curzulae
(in *M.H.S.M.*), cap. xxxv. p. 15. "Si quis mercatur emendo
aliquid ab aliquo dederit unum denarium parvum pro arris,
mercator sit firmum et venditor teneatur dare et emptor recipere
merces: ab uno denario supra si aliquis dederit arras, pro quo
remanebit mercatum, ille teneatur solvere alteri parti arras in
duplum." Cf. p. 36, cap. 38.

1302. Florence. St. Calimalae, Lb. iii. cap. i. "Quo denario
dato mercatum stabile sit et firmum."

1312. Spalati vetus statutum, Lb. iii. cap. 96, p. 109 (in
M.H.S.M.). "Si...arre date fuerint...dictum mercatum sit firmum
et ratum...quia nihil tam contingit fidei humane congruum quam
ea que juste per pactum inter aliquos intervenerunt observari."

14th century. St. Scardonae (in *M.H.S.M.*), cap. x. p. 122.
"Si aliquas arras dederit, illud mercatum nec emptor nec venditor
valeat relinquere."

[2] 1347.   Lattes, *Diritto Commerciale*, p. 132, note 14.
"Quando le merci fossero state spalmate o benedicte, chi mancava
al contratto dovesse risarcire ogni danno, invece se si fosse
soltanto data la caparra, chi l' aveva dato dovesse perderla, chi l'
aveva ricevuta, restituire il doppio." Quoted from St. de Varisio.

[3] Brunneck, *Siciliens Mittelalterliche Stadtrechte*, p. 186,
note 1.

penalty for breach of contract until a law of
Frederick II. forbade the custom.   There are signs
of the same uncertainty in Germany.   At Hildesheim[1],
in the middle of the 13th century, the Earnest did
not make the contract binding, while according to
the custumal of 1300 it did.

Maritime Law again, which showed great uniformity in later times, was far from uniform during
the Middle Ages.   Numerous local laws and customs
existed which were gradually supplanted in the
North by the Laws of Oleron and Wisby, and in the
South by the Laws of Barcelona.   It was a slow
process, however, for as late as the 17th century the
code of Amalfi[2] was recognised in Southern Italy,
while legislation in England, Holland and France
soon began to create fresh divergences.

But it is perhaps in the fairs, where special
courts existed for administering the Law Merchant,
that strict uniformity might most naturally be
expected; for here the international element was
unusually strong.   Foreigners are judged in the Fair
Court of St Ives[3]; Spanish, Italian, French and

---

[1] 1249. Stadtrecht of Hildesheim, cap. 23. (In *Hildesheim
Urkundenbuch*, vol. i. no. 209.)   "Si quis aliquid emerit et aliquam summam super eo dederit quod dicitur 'oringe,' si idem vult
retractet ipse amittet summam quam dederit; si vero venditor
retractare voluerit, ipse summam quam accepit restituet et postea
duplo restituet ipsam summam que dicitur 'oringe.'"

Circa 1300. Stadtrecht, cap. 152, no. 548, p. 294.   "Koft
me enne kop und gift me dar enne goddespenning up, de kop
scal stede sin."

[2] v. Wagner, *Seerecht*, p. 37, note 7.

[3] v. cases in court of St Ives. Maitland, *Select Pleas*, pp. 152,
155.

German merchants are among the contracting parties in the bonds of the Fair of Ypres[1], while to the great Fairs of Champagne merchants streamed from every part of Europe. But even in fairs there is evidence to show that the Law is not everywhere identical. When Edward I. declared in the Carta Mercatoria that all plaints of foreigners should be decided according to the Law Merchant, he added that if any dispute should arise as to their contracts with any persons, proof and inquiry should be made according to the usages and customs of the fairs and market towns where the contract had been made[2]. Evidently the usages and customs of fairs differed. Equally significant is the statute of Westminster of 1275. " It is ordained," ran one of its clauses, " that in any city, borough town, fair or market, a foreign person who is of this realm shall not be distrained for any debt for which he is not debtor or pledge." This changed the law as observed in English towns and fairs, and created a difference between the usage in England and in other countries. In Northern Italy a long series[3] of treaties—many of later date

---

[1] Des Marez, *La Lettre de foire à Ypres.* See documents, nos. 68, 73, 74, 77, 81, 84.

[2] *Monumenta Gildhallae,* II. i. p. 206. " Et si forsan super contractu hujusmodi contentio oriatur, fiat inde probatio vel inquisitio secundum usus et consuetudines feriarum et villarum mercatoriarum ubi dictum contractum fieri contigerit et iniri."

[3] See the many treaties printed in *I trattati commerciali della Repubblica Fiorentina* by Arias. The treaty of 1279 included all Venice, Genoa, and all the cities of Tuscany, Lombardy and Romagna. Fairs are not specially mentioned, but the terms of the treaty are so general as to include them. This treaty provided that " nullus dictarum civitatum possit vel debeat pro

than Edward's legislation—was slowly and fitfully
securing for the Italians this same protection against
distraint for the debts of a fellow-citizen. The law,
however, for long remained unchanged and. in the
case of absence or repudiation of a treaty, the
Italian had no protection.

In England it seems that at one time the procedure adopted in fairs and towns against absent
defendants varied so much that a 14th century
treatise on the "Lex Mercatoria[1]" declared that no
one could know or ascertain the procedure of the
Law Merchant on this point. Uniformity in this
particular was, however, established in the end, and
probably with the aid of the royal authority[2].

Still, in spite of minor differences, the international character of the Law Merchant as
administered in the fair courts cannot be denied.
"The customs of different places may have varied
slightly, but the law in its broad lines was necessarily
of that international character which has always
been its chief characteristic." Nor is this true only
of the law administered in fairs. The same general

---

alio detineri vel capi vel etiam inquietari in persona vel rebus,
sed cui datum fuerit illi solum requiratur vel illi qui de jure
teneretur." Arias, p. 402.

[1] Bickley, *The Little Red Book of Bristol*, p. 62. "Et ita
diversimode in diversis partibus quod nullus omnino processum
legis mercatorie in ea parte scire nec cognoscere poterit."

[2] Bickley, *The Little Red Book of Bristol*, p. 62. The new
uniform regulations which are evidently intended to apply to the
whole kingdom are introduced by "propter hoc ordinatum est."
Uniformity was secured not by custom, but by regulation from
above.

agreement upon the main rules and principles, with
the same divergences upon less important points,
characterize all the commercial codes and customs of
Europe. The Law Merchant, in fact, was vague and
indefinite; in many of its courts the law was
regarded as a purely customary law to be declared,
in case of doubt, by the merchants of the courts
themselves, and even where its rules had been codified
there were in reserve unwritten rules founded on
custom which the commercial judges were ordered to
observe[1]. But in spite of its vagueness the Law

[1] A.D. 1281. St. of Como in *Monumenta Historiae Patriae*,
vol. XVI. column 15. "Eadem [placita] definiam...secundum
statuta pertinentia ad officium mercatorum, et deficientibus ipsis
statutis secundum alia statuta consulum Cumarum justiciae et
civitatis Cumarum, deficientibus ipsis secundum usus et bonos
mores civitatis ejusdem approbatos, et his deficientibus secundum
leges et jura."

1305. Pisa. *Breve Curiae Mercatorum*, c. 9. (Bonaini,
vol. III. p. 12.) "Et si qua reclamatio coram me...de minori
quantitate solidorum XL denariorum fuerit facta ipsam diffiniam...
secundum usum pisanae civitatis et consuetudinem mercatorum."

1305. *Eodem*, c. 6, p. 10. "Si constitutum inde non
est in causa hujus, secundum bonum usum civitatis Pisanae et
mercatantie."

1305. *Eodem*, c. 81, p. 59. "Et juro quod observabo et
tenebo omnes et singulas bonas consuetudines et bonos usus
quae et qui fieri consueverunt in suprascripta curia in terminando
lites et causas."

1250. St. Bologna of 1250, Lb. iv. cap. 19 a. "Quod jus
fori et mercati reddatur secundum consuetudinem fori sive
mercati."

1237. Commercial Treaty between Florence and Sien (Arias,
op. cit. 373). "Teneantur arbitri...omnes lites...diffinire...secun-
dum jura et bonum usum mercantiae utriusque terrae."

1400. St. Merc. Mantuae, c. 2. "Omnes lamentationes et
querimonias mihi factas a meis negociatoribus diffiniam secundum

Merchant existed. In every commercial country in Europe there were rules and legal doctrines for merchants and mercantile transactions that were regarded alike by merchants and by jurists as distinct from the common law of the land.

These rules and doctrines, which were distinct, it must be repeated, from the common law, were the Law Merchant. Each country, it may almost be said each town, had its own variety of Law Merchant, yet all were but varieties of the same species. Everywhere the leading principles and the most important rules were the same, or tended to become the same. It is the growth and development of these common rules and underlying principles that constitute the history of the Law Merchant. No doubt, in each country the Law Merchant to a certain

rationem et bonam consuetudinem negociacionis et secundum statutum mercadandiae."

1161. Prologue to *Constitutum usus* of Pisa (Bonaini, vol. II. and Pertile, I. p. 395, note 35). "Pisana itaque civitas propter conversationem diversarum gentium per diversas mundi partes, suas consuetudines non scriptas habere meruit, super quas annuatim judices posuit, quos previsores appellavit, ut ex equitate pro salute justitiae, et honore et salvamento civitatis, tam civibus quam advenis et peregrinis et omnibus universaliter in consuetudinibus praeviderent....Unde Pisani...consuetudines suas quas propter conversationem quam cum diversis gentibus habuerunt, et huc usque in memoriam retinuerunt, in scriptis statuerunt redigendas, pro cognitione omnium ea scire volentium."

It is to be noted that of the five "previsores" only one was to be a jurisperitus, and that a copy of the "constitutum usus" was always to be in the "curia maris" for any one belonging to the Sea Gild (aliquis de ordine maris) to consult. See Schaube, *Das Consulat des Meeres in Pisa*, pp. 127 and 129.

extent traced out its own curve of progress. The English Law Merchant has its history, no less than the Italian. But neither alone is the history of the Law Merchant. This essay has for its object to trace the development of the common essential elements that are found in the early Law Merchant of every country. The scope of the subject is not narrow and I can only attempt briefly to touch upon what seem the most important points.

The Law Merchant, then, was a body of rules and principles relating to merchants and mercantile transactions, distinct from the ordinary law of the land. Possessed of a certain uniformity in its essential features, it yet differed on minor points from' place to place. The question at once arises, in what did this uniformity of character consist? To this question only a close investigation can give a complete answer, but the essential features of the Law Merchant and the broad general principles that permanently influenced its development, are clearly marked and can be stated at the outset.

In the first place, the Law Merchant was in the main customary law. "The grandeur and significance of the medieval merchant," says Goldschmidt, "is that he creates his own laws out of his own needs and his own views." Early in the 11th century, the German merchants were already asserting the force of their own customs against the common law. "Merchants assert," said Notker[1],

---

[1] Keutgen, *Urkunden*, no. 74, p. 44. "Also choufliute stritent, tas der chouf sule wesen state, der ze jarmercate getan wurdet, er si reht alde unreht, wanda iz iro gewoneheite ist."

"that sales made in fairs, whether made with proper legal forms or not, should be binding, since it is their custom." A few years later the merchants of Tiel[1] are described as deciding cases not according to the law, but as they wished. In Italy the commercial judges based their decisions upon custom and upon mercantile statutes[2] framed for the most part by the Merchant Gild, though confirmed by the State. The Bristol Treatise[3] on the Lex Mercatoria shows clearly that in England the force of custom was recognised. Everywhere, in commercial transactions, custom held sway, and even where the State legislated it had often merely to confirm or slightly modify the rules that had long before been established by custom.

The earliest English statute on Insurance, of the year 1601, declares that it "hathe been tyme out of mynde an usage among merchants," while similarly

---

[1] Keutgen, A.D. 1018, *Urkunden*, no. 75. "Judicia non secundum legem sed secundum voluntatem decernentes." Cf. Freiburg Stadtrecht of 1120 (Keutgen, no. 133, c. 5, p. 118). "Disceptatio...pro consuetudinario et legitimo jure omnium mercatorum, praecipue autem Coloniensium examinabitur judicio."

[2] v. quotations, pp. 8, 9.

[3] In *Little Red Book of Bristol*, vol. I. c. 4, p. 60. "Sed apponitur adhuc le affidavit propter antiquam consuetudinem."

c. 21, p. 83. "Ut ipsi...fieri facerent quod de jure et secundum legem et consuetudinem mercatoriam fuerit faciendum."

For maritime law cf. *Black Book of Admiralty*, p. 3. The Admiral is to appoint as deputies "Some of the most loyal, wise and discreete persons in the law maratime and ancient customs of the sea."

Black Book of Admiralty, vol. I. p. 168. Additions to *Inquisition of Queensborough*, cap. 71. "Est de faire sommaire et plain proces selon loy marine et ancienne coustume de la mer." Cf. p. 409.

on the Continent the early statutes dealing with insurance only legislated upon minor points, leaving the main points to be decided by custom[1]. "In all great matters relating to commerce the legislators have copied, not dictated."

This customary nature of the Law Merchant was by far the most decisive factor in its development: it made the law eminently a practical law adapted to the requirements of commerce; and as trade expanded and new forms of commercial activity arose —negotiable paper, insurance, etc.—custom everywhere fashioned and framed the broad general principles of the new law. Custom is alike the ruling principle and the originating force of the Law Merchant.

The summary nature of its jurisdiction is a second feature that always characterised the Lex Mercatoria. Its justice was prompt, its procedure summary, and often the time within which disputes must be finally settled was narrowly limited[2]. To

---

[1] Goldschmidt, *Handbuch des Handelsrecht*, pp. 374—5, 378—9.

[2] 12th cent. Rouen. *Établissements*, c. 26. "Si quis requis-erit curiam suam de debitis, conceditur ei, et faciat rectum clamius in *duabus octonis*."

The customs of Rouen were received in many French cities. See Gory's edition.

1302. Florence. St. Calimalae, Lb. ii. c. 2. "Et teneantur consules finire et terminare hujusmodi quaestiones...intra *XL.* dies."

12th cent. Pisa. *Constitutum usus*, c. 11. "Et post quam liquet, infra *octo* dies eam diffiniat."

1305. Pisa. *Breve Maris*, c. 19. "Omnes causas infra *tertium* diem ex quo mihi liquebit...diffiniam, nisi justa causa remanserit."

prevent lengthy processes it is not rare to find appeals forbidden[1]. Speedy justice, in fact, was necessary for merchants, and while the Canon Law[2] and the usage of the Papal Chancery may have furthered the development of this summary procedure in the Law Merchant, there can be no doubt that it was mainly due to the necessity experienced by the merchants themselves[3] of a speedy settlement of their disputes. This characteristic feature of the Law Merchant seems especially to have struck the 14th century author of the Bristol Treatise. " The _ex Mercati," he remarks, "differs from the common

1400. St. Merc. Mantuae, c. 2. " Omnes lamentationes et querimonias...occasione mercadandiae diffiniam et determinabo infra *unum mensem*."

1286. St. of Como. Cases " inter mercatores occasione mercationum " to be decided "infra xv dies utiles," between other persons " infra duos menses."

[1] 1286. *Breve Pisani communis*, Lb. i. c. 61 (Bonaini, i. p. 155). "Omnes sententiae quae feruntur a consulibus ordinis maris de naulo et mariuatico et de avere guasto, a libris centum infra valeant...a quibus sententiis non possit appellari."

See numerous references in Lattes, *Diritto Commerciale*, p. 279, note 59.

[2] 1306. The Decretal " Clementina Saepe " of Clement VI. dealt with the summary procedure, and there is a striking analogy in substance and form between the language of the Italian Statutes and the Decretal. See Lattes, *Studii di diritto statuario*, p. 51.

[3] Goldschmidt quotes (p. 174) from St. Merc. of Verona (p. 114).

1406. " More mercationis expedite et breviter procedatur, quia bene scitis quod mercatorum conditio longitudines non requirat." Cf. Bonaini, iii. 207 note.

1384. " Si mercatorum negotia ad litigatorum tergiversationes et judicales observantias reducantur, peribit de societate mortalium mercatura."

law of the realm in three ways; in the first place[1]
'quod celerius deliberat se ipsam.' 'The plees,' says
the Domesday Book of Ipswich[2], 'betwixe straunge
folk that men clepeth pypoudrous shouldene ben
pleted from day to day if the pleyntiff or the de-
fendaunt preye of suche aiourning. The plees in
time of fair betwixe straunge and passant shouldene
beene pleted from hour to hour as well in the fore-
noon as afternoon......and the plees yoven to the
law maryne, that is to wit for straunge maryners
passant and for hem that abyden not but her tyde
should be pleted from tide to tide.'" The desire tu
despatch expressed itself in many ways but everywhere the principle is evident. In Italy[3] almost all
the commercial statutes of the various cities instructed

---

[1] *Lex Mercatoria*, c. 2.

[2] *Black Book of Admiralty*, vol. ii. pp. 22, 23.

[3] St. of Brescia (1313), Lb. iii. c. 59 (*Monumenta Historiae Patriae*, vol. xvi. column 1737). The "consules mercatorum" in cases "de mercatis et rebus mobilibus pertinentibus ad mercathendiam" are to proceed "summarie sine porrectione libelli et litis contestione et sine strepitu juditiorum, ita quod processus...valeat et teneat ac si rigor juris esset solemniter et integre observatus."

A.D. 1403—7. *Leges Genuenses* (edited by Poggi in *M.H.P.*, column 537).

1403—7. "Causae quae inter mercatores Januenses orientur causa mercandi...magistratus teneatur...diffinire summarie et de plano sine strepitu et figura judicii."

1302. Florence. St. Calimalae, Lb. ii. c. 2. "Sine contestione litis et qualibet juris solemnitate strepituque judicii." (Also in Italian version of 1332.)

See numerous references in Lattes, *Diritto Commerciale*, p. 267, note 2.

the judges to use a summary procedure. At Pisa[1] it was in maritime law at first confined to a limited number of cases, but in the later statutes of the city the procedure gradually gained ground. At Marseilles[2], where the existence of commercial judges dates from the 12th century, it was their duty to decide cases and disputes between merchants "summarily, without regard to the subtleties of the law." The German Hanse, the English and French Admiralty all administered summary justice[3]. For the passing stranger or the foreign merchant *en route*, a specially prompt justice was generally the

[1] 1248. "Quaestio marinariatici et nauli, et de mercibus amissis seu deterioratis in navi...summatim...dirimatur" (*Constitutum usus*, c. 11).

1259. "De mercedibus hominum et vecturis animalium idem observatur."

1281. "Potestas...de litibus...contra magistros lignaminum et murorum et contra alios opifices pro eorum artificio, debeat summatim...cognoscere et eas finire infra 8 dies."

1286. "Si inter creditores de bonis obligatis aut ypoteca bonorum quaestio fuerit, summatim de plano, etc."

v. Pertile, vol. vi. ii. p. 116, note 10. Schaube (*Das Consulat des Meeres in Pisa*) deals fully with this development of summary procedure in Pisa, pp. 135—6.

[2] See Morel, *Les Juridictions Commerciales au Moyen Age*, pp. 135—7.

[3] *Black Book of Admiralty*, p. 409. It was the duty of the deputy of the English High Admiral "to make summary and hasty process from tide to tide according to the ancient law marine and ancient customs of the sea without observing the solemnity of the law." For French admiralty see ordonnance of 1373 (in *Black Book of Admiralty*, p. 480), "Sera tenue la juridiction du dit admiral...de jour en jour et d'heure en autre."

rule[1]; it was felt that the usual procedure, prompt as it was, did not meet their case.

Thirdly, the Law Merchant was characterized by the spirit of equity. In the 18th century an English judge[2] spoke of the Lex Mercatoria as "a system of equity founded on rules of equity and governed in all its parts by plain justice and good faith." " In the plaints (causis) of merchants," declare the Gild Statutes of Bergamo for 1457, "equity is especially to be considered and the cases are to be decided 'ex aequo et bono'; it is not meet to dispute on the subtleties of the Law." At Aquila[3] the consuls (1396) were to inquire into " the pure and simple truth, as the usage and equity of merchants demanded, and

---

[1] Grimm, *Rechtsalterthümer*, I. 556. "Keme ein fremder man und begehrte ein notgericht, dem soll man unverzogenliche gehorsam sein."

c. 1200. St. Antiqua Merc. Placentiae, c. 633. "Consules mercadandie debeant facere cuilibet foresterio conquerenti de aliquo civitatis et districtus summariam et brevissimam rationem."

1214. St. Cuzulae (in *M.H.S.M.*, p. 35), cap. 35. "Si viatores...forenses contra homines insulae placitare voluerint de aliqua ratione eodem die contracta, homo insulae teneatur sibi statim sine aliquo termino respondere; et si ille forensis traheret hic moram, respondeat sibi usque ad duos dies et sicut homo insulae tenetur forensibus respondere." (Confirmed 1265, p. 15, c. 32.)

1312. St. vetus Spalati (in *M.H.S.M.*), c. 5, p. 9. "Quaestiones forensium mercatorum possint etiam quocunque tempore agitari tam in dictis festivitatibus et diebus feriatis quam et non feriatis......ut possint sine morà et dilatione aliqua expediri."

Cf. Domesday of Ipswich, and Silberschmidt, *Die Entstehung des deutschen Handelsgerichts*, p. 31.

[2] Buller, J., in Master *v.* Miller (4 T.R., 320).

[3] 1395. Muratori, *Antiq. Ital.*, VI. 788, quoted by Pertile, VII. p. 114, note 9.

as it was wont to be done in mercantile actions and affairs," and the consuls of Bologna (1279) gave judgment "secundum quod aequum crediderint[1]." In Venice by a decree of the Council (1287) the consuls of the merchants were to swear to decide disputes according to custom, and if custom failed them, "secundum bonam conscientiam[2]." At Marseilles[3] the same spirit prevailed and the judges were to decide suits between merchants "sans s'atteindre aux subtilités des lois et des ordonnances[3]." England, however, lagged behind. It was mainly an agricultural, not a commercial country, and its commercial jurisprudence developed slowly. The records of the Fair Court of St Ives[4] show that formalism and technicalities still held their ground. Verbal

[1] 1279. Stat. Mercat. Florent. Bon., quoted by Pertile, vi. i. p. 113, note 8.

[2] 1287. Quoted by Lattes, *Il Diritto Commerciale*, p. 78, note 1.

1302. St. Calimalae, Lb. ii. c. 2. "Item quod in quaestionibus xxv. librarum vel infra consules possint procedere in cognoscendo et sententiendo ad eorum arbitrium et voluntatem."

1305. Pisa. St. Mercatorum, c. 81 (Bonaini, iii. 59). "Possimus nos consules...cognoscere diffinire et arbitrari praecipere quidquid nobis...*videbitur aequum* de omnibus et singulis erroribus et dolis et fraudibus."

1384. Letter from Signoria of Florence to commune of Pisa (Bonaini, iii. 207). "Hanc autem litem audivimus non aequitate mercatoria discuti, sed ad judiciorum calumnias coartari......sed *in aequitate mercatoria* visa simplici veritate sine morae dispendio dirimatur."

[3] Edict of 1565. "Ont été créés et institués *de toute ancienneté* par le conseil de la ville deux juges des marchands pour juger et décider......Sans s'atteindre *aux subtilités des lois* et des ordonnances." Quoted by Morel, *op. cit.*, p. 136.

[4] Maitland, *Select Pleas in Manorial Courts*, 136.

accuracy was required of the defendant and it was possible for a debtor to defraud his creditor and prevent attachment of his goods by going through the farce of a mock sale. An equitable procedure, however, was in English towns slowly supplanting the old system. The Leicester Charter[1] of 1277 may be taken as an example. "Whereas," declares the preamble, "the delays of the Portmanmoot of Leicester have been too long and some usages have injured those who had to sue their right, Sir Edmund, Lord of the aforesaid town,......by his council and by the assent of the Mayor and the Jurates and the whole community of the same town, has ordered and provided the amendments underwritten. In the first place because it happened that when a man impleaded another for debts or trespass, half a year or a whole year often passed before he could bring his adversary to answer, partly by reason of the feeble distress of the bailiffs, and partly because men hid their goods in rooms or elsewhere, so that no one could distrain them......let order to distrain be issued to make him attend the Third Court by the great distress by whatsoever may be found of his within his house or without, so that if he causes his goods to be hidden or shut up in a room or elsewhere, the bailiff by view of the neighbours may enter everywhere to distrain him till justice be done......And whereas it was customary heretofore when the parties ought to plead and the plaintiff had said his plaint, if the defendant directly the plea had left the plaintiff's mouth did not say 'Thwerthutnay' he

[1] Bateson, *Records of Leicester*, i. 150.

was held to be non-defendant, and that was called
Swarless, and he was not allowed to plead nor to ask
council nor have any man who knew the usages to
speak for him, whereby many from not knowing the
usages lost their suits: for this it is now provided,
that when the parties appear and ought to plead,
let the plaintiff fully state his case, without challenge
or hindrance, by himself, if he knows how, or if not
by another who is avowed, so that the suit shall not
be abated by non-specification of time or by any
other circumstances challenged.   But if the defendant demands declaration of time or other thing
necessary to the plaint that he may be better certain
of answering, let the declaration be made at the same
time without challenge......And if he trow that his
first answer does not suffice, let him say something
else to which he is willing to hold absolutely and upon
which he will take judgment......And whereas it was
heretofore the custom that the defendant could not
answer any other thing to the plaintiff's plea except
to admit everything or to say fully a 'thwart-nay,'
and when he had said the nay, he had to be at his
law himself the sixth hand (*i.e.*, to find five com-
purgators), then the plaintiff or a man for him
would choose folk that would not go with him for
favour of the other party or for hatred of him, and if
he could not make his law with the folk named, he
would be attainted of the whole plea, whether it
were true or false.   Therefore it is provided, first
that in plea of debt if the defendant denies it and
the demandant has proved his debt by writing, tally
or by word of mouth, let him be received to make

the proof, so that if he had nothing but tally or word of mouth, let him swear first and then his witness whom he brings be examined of the hearing and of the sight, if they were at the taking of the debt or the making of the tally or if they were at the place where the debt or the tally was granted from, and according to what they prove let him recover or lose his debt." Equally reasonable are the customs of Bristol[1] in "pleas of debts, contracts and covenants," during the 14th century, while in the 15th century the Admiralty expressly acknowledges the principle of equity. It was the duty of the deputy of the High Admiral[2] "to make summary and hasty process from tide to tide according to the ancient law marine and ancient customs of the sea without observing the solemnity of the law and without mixing the law civil with the law maritime, there where it may be equitable, knowing the rights of the parties." Plain justice and good faith, disregard of technicalities and regard for "the sole truth of the matter," characterize alike in England, France, and Italy, the development of the Law Merchant.

But perhaps the most striking feature of the Law Merchant is its strongly marked international character. The main lines of development were everywhere the same, and by it foreigners were generally judged. Its rules and regulations have their origin in many lands. Pisan Laws[3] passed into

---

[1] Bickley, *Little Red Book of Bristol*, p. 40. Consuetudines, c. 31.

[2] *Black Book of Admiralty*, i. 409.

[3] Wagner, *Seerecht*, p. 39, note 11.

the sea code of Marseilles.   Oleron and Lubeck gave laws to the North of Europe, Barcelona to the South; while from Italy came the legal principle of insurance and bills of exchange.

The international nature of the sources from which it drew its rules and of the persons over whom it exercised jurisdiction, combined with the universality of its guiding principles, fairly entitle the Law Merchant to be called " the private international law of the Middle Ages[1]."

---

[1] Maitland, *Select Pleas in Manorial Courts*, 133.

CHAPTER II.

THE RISE OF THE LAW MERCHANT.

THE origin of the Law Merchant, that is, of a special law for merchants and their business transactions, is closely connected with the history of commerce, fairs and markets during the troubled centuries that followed the fall of the Western Empire. Slowly during this period market and fair became an administrative and judicial unit distinct from the rest of the land, and this development is of great importance in the history of commercial law.

In the Merovingian Empire the whole land, market, fair and open country, was under the same administration. The series of charters[1] (629—759) relating to the fair of St Denis shows that the fair depended for justice and order upon the ordinary royal officials, the count and hundredman who drew no legal distinction between peasant and merchant or market and the open country. To the merchant the Merovingian Empire offered no special protection. From the Carlovingian rulers, however, merchants and commerce received more consideration.

[1] Huvelin, *Droit des Marchés*, 146—7.

Grants and confirmations of markets and fairs grew more numerous, and the crown began to place the merchants under its special protection. "You have written to us about your merchants," says Charlemagne in a letter to Offa, King of Mercia; "we would have them enjoy our protection and defence within our realm according to the ancient custom in commerce, and if in any place they are distressed by unjust oppression, let them appeal to us and we will order justice to be done. Show the same favour to our merchants." The royal protection was even granted to individual merchants, who had however generally to pay for the privilege. Jurisdiction still remained in the hands of the royal officials, but under the later Carlovingian monarchs a decisive change took place and jurisdiction over markets and fairs began to be granted to the local lords. Concessions of immunity, especially to churches and monasteries, grew common, and created a kind of preserve into which the judicial officers of the crown had no right to enter [1]. Even more important is the fact that the charters, granting to nobles or ecclesiastical foundations rights of market or fair, now contain, as a general rule, the concession of the ban, which carried with it the right of jurisdiction— "Cum omni judiciaria potestate, hoc est bannum [2]." But it was in Germany, especially during the 10th and 11th centuries, that fairs and markets were founded in greatest number and the charters are most instructive. In the first place they regularly

---

[1] Huvelin, *Droit des Marchés*, 160.
[2] *op. cit.* 171, vide 168—172.

grant in the plainest terms to the local lord jurisdiction over the market and freedom from the judicial
interference of the royal official. " We ordain," says
the market charter[1] of Meppen for the year 946,
"that no public judge shall exercise any judicial
power in the aforesaid place save the lawful advocate
of the aforesaid abbot." Similarly the charter of
Stade fair (1038) granted to the Archbishop of
Hamburg " potestatem constringendi omnes qui
illuc convenerint ad omnem justiciam faciendam[2]."
Market and fair were freeing themselves for judicial purposes from the direct control of the central
power, and by the 13th century the process was
complete. "In our presence," declared[3] Frederick
II in 1218," judgment has been given by the princes
and magnates of our empire that if we have by
charter conferred on any one a fair or weekly market
the Count or other judge of that province has there no
jurisdiction or power of punishing offences." In Italy
and England the feudal lords had won the same
right of jurisdiction. " I grant and concede," says a
Neapolitan charter of 1115, "to the said monastery
and its abbots the rights of administering justice in
civil cases which may arise during the aforesaid
days" of the fair. As early as the 9th century a
monastery of Piacenza was granted the jurisdiction
over a newly founded fair, "homines quoque qui
ad ipsum mercatum occurrerint, si in aliquo devi-

---

[1] Keutgen, *Urkunden zur städtischen Verfassungsgeschichte*,
no. 39.

[2] *op. cit.*, no. 57.

[3] *op. cit.*, no. 66.

averint, a ministris ipsius monasterii distringantur
et de transgressione justitiam perficiant[1]." In
France not merely the jurisdiction over fairs but
the right of founding them had passed into the
hands of the feudal lords and it was not till the
13th century that the crown was able to recover the
exclusive right of creating a new fair.

The second point that the early charters show is
that the special protection of the merchant by the
crown had been extended to all merchants on their
journeys to and from market or fair. "They may found
a public market," says the Meppen charter (946),
" and those coming, returning and dwelling there shall
have firm-stablished peace as our royal predecessors
have long ago granted to the other public places of
merchants." A special penalty safeguarded merchants
and market. " By our imperial power," ran a clause in
the Helsmarshauser charter (997)[2], "we ordain that
all traders and others using the market, tarrying there
or coming or returning, shall have such peace and
such justice as those who trade at Mainz, Cologne
and Dortmund, and those who infringe or disturb
the market shall pay the same penalty."

From at least the 9th century onward the merchants were a class distinguished from the rest of the
community by legal privileges that gave them a
protection which others did not share, while market
and fair formed a separate judicial unit which no
royal judge could enter. From the very nature of
the case this separate jurisdiction tended in the

---

[1] Pertile, *Storia del Diritto Italiano*, III. 505, note 373.
[2] Keutgen, *Urkunden*, no. 50 b.

absence of strong control from the central authority
to adapt itself to the requirements of commerce and
industry which in fair and market were the all-
important elements. The establishment of isolated
jurisdictions did not necessarily imply the employment of new law, but the gradual adoption of rules
adapted to their special requirements was not only
possible, but natural. The circumstances were
favourable for the growth in market and fair of a
special law for merchants and a special law arose.
But it is not till the end of the 10th century when
these favourable circumstances were well established
that there is conclusive evidence that special rules
existed.

The evidence of Notker and the reference to the
customary law of the merchants of Tiel date from the
commencement of the 11th century. Earlier evidence
than this does not seem to exist. There is indeed
a clause in the Bremen charter of 965 which
may possibly refer to a special law for merchants
—"negotiatores......potiantur jure quali ceterarum
regalium institores urbium[1]." "Jure " however is an
ambiguous term and may here only refer, as it often
does elsewhere, to privileges such as freedom from toll
or protection against violence. However this may be,
special rules for deciding mercantile transactions
existed in the 11th century and cannot be proved to
exist earlier than the middle of the 10th[2] century.

---

[1] Keutgen, no. 7.

[2] Cf. case referred to by Huvelin, p. 194, and Sohm, *Die
Entstehung des deutschen Städtewesen*, 54. The time is the reign
of Charles the Bald. Two merchants have sold goods in common;

The rise of this special law coincided with the establishment of conditions highly favourable to the evolution of a special law for commerce. It is only natural to conclude that it is to these favourable conditions—the rise of local jurisdictions in markets and fairs free from the effective control of the central power and the existence of a merchant class distinct from the general mass of the population—that the origin of the Law Merchant is due.

In every country where commerce is of any importance the law must be adapted to the requirements of trade, but where the central power is strong and the judicial organisation uniform and under control, the adaptation need merely modify the common law of the land and need not create a separate system of law. In times and countries however where the central power is weak and the merchant and his disputes appear before courts secure from all effective control, the growth of a separate law may be expected. It does not seem too much to say that out of the immunity of market and fair courts rose the Law Merchant.

In the development of the Law Merchant the towns played an important, perhaps the most important part. The special law that had arisen in market

one of them receives payment and refuses to give the other his share. "Contentione oborta, judex fori E. vocabulo, occurrit, cumque litem dirimere vellet, atque ille, qui pretium habuerat, compari se reddidisse omnibus modis affirmaret, nec dictis ejus fides adhiberetur, necessitate compulsus, dexteram contra basilicam extendens cum furo juramentum protulit." The case is curious, and it is difficult to decide whether we have here a special method of procedure.

and fair was transferred to the town. " If any dispute
arise between my burghers," says the Freiburg charter[1]
of 1120, " it shall not be decided according to my
will or the will of their rector, but by the customary
and legitimate law of all merchants and especially by
the law of the merchants of Cologne." The Law
Merchant became a part of the Law of the Town, and
in Germany the theory has been advanced that in
town law it was at first the all-important element
from which the law of the town sprang[2]. According
to this view the Law Merchant was the origin of
town law, which was in its broad features merely an
expansion and development of the special law of
merchants. The theory has been disputed and for
the early history of Law Merchant it is not of vital
importance. It is sufficient that the Law Merchant
became an integral part of the Law of the Town and
of this fact there is no doubt. In every land during
the 12th and following centuries the towns begin to
record their laws and customs, which everywhere
contain legal rules for commerce that differ from the
common law of the land. For the development of
the Law Merchant this reception of the law by
the towns was of decisive importance. It was the
period of the rise of towns to wealth and greatness
and of the growth of their rights of self-government.
The Law Merchant had now a wider sphere of activity.
It was no longer confined to occasional fairs and
markets but had found a permanent abode.

In the great commercial cities of Southern Europe

[1] Keutgen, no. 133, c. 5, p. 118.
[2] Sohm and others.

trade was now on a far vaster scale and far more
complex than it had been in the fairs and markets
of the 9th and 10th centuries; and as commerce
developed so did the Law Merchant. Everywhere the
Law Merchant showed signs of progress, but in every
country the progress was not the same. For in the
main the development of the law was determined by
the expansion of commerce and the growth of rights
of self-government in the various cities, and these
conditions were not satisfied everywhere to the same
degree.

In Italy the cities of Lombardy and Tuscany
were from the 11th century onward practically
independent republics, while at the same time their
trade advanced by leaps and bounds. The bulk of
the trade between Europe and the East was in their
hand; they had their settlements in Constantinople
and the Levant. There was here free scope for the
rise of new customs and for the development of
commercial law. The cities of Italy realised that
commerce and industry were the sources of their
power and wealth, and to increase commerce and
industry was the main object of their policy. Their
independent position gave them a free hand and
enabled them to adopt those rules and regulations
that seemed best adapted to the requirements of
trade. Under these favourable circumstances commercial law developed rapidly. Rules and customs
multiplied and it was soon found necessary to commit
the old customary law to writing. More completely
than elsewhere the Law Merchant in Italy ceased to
be a purely customary law and began to change into

a Lex Scripta. It was a great change, but it is easy to exaggerate both its completeness and its importance. The Law did not become a purely statutory law, for the commercial statutes made no claim to completeness. The force of old unrecorded customs was expressly recognised and new customs were constantly forming.

As original authorities for the early history of the Law Merchant the Italian commercial statutes are invaluable; they throw a flood of light upon the origin and development of commercial rules and customs that then or afterwards found their way into the commercial laws of Europe. So long as the Law Merchant remained a customary law, unwritten and unrecorded in statutes or codes, almost the only original sources were scattered references in charters and contemporary histories. But in neither charter nor historian is detailed information to be found. Their evidence is indeed sufficient to prove that a special law existed, but it is impossible from them alone to form a full and comprehensive view of what the rules and doctrines of the Law Merchant in early times really were. The rarity through Europe of early records of the fair and market courts makes the evidence of the Italian statutes all the more valuable. A striking feature of these Italian statutes is their length and completeness. The merchant gild regulations of Piacenza which run into several hundred paragraphs and the elaborate Pisan "constitutum usus" date in part from the 12th century. In no other country can be found such ample information of such early date upon the customs and regulations that

prevailed among merchants.   Nor do the Pisan and
Piacenza laws stand alone.   For the 13th and 14th
centuries there exist for almost every city of
importance in Northern Italy collections of commercial statutes that give a full and detailed account
of the commercial law that was observed within the
city[1].   The history of their formation requires
examination[2].

In most, though not in all of the Italian cities
commercial law is to be found mainly in the statutes
of the merchant gilds.   In Italy, as elsewhere, the
gilds were allowed a large measure of self-government
and framed their own regulations, which merely
required to be confirmed by the governing body of
the city.   These regulations were subject to constant
revision and emendation, and in many of the gilds
there were special and often permanent officials—
the emendatores—whose duty it was to revise the
statutes and suggest alterations.   Their proposals
needed to be confirmed by the general council of the
gild and by the city authorities.   It would be a
mistake however to regard these regulations, in spite
of their origin, as gild statutes pure and simple.
Once confirmed, tacitly or expressly, they had all the
authority of state law, binding upon all who traded
within the city[3].   No doubt at first their application
was limited to members of the gild, but, as will be

---

[1] v. Lattes, *Il Diritto Commerciale nella Legislazione Statuaria*.

[2] *op. cit.*, paragraph 4, pp. 57—70.

[3] Gild Statutes of Bergamo, cap. xxx. "Magnifici Potestates et
Rectores Pergami praesentes et futuri eorumque judices, aliique
jus dicentes in Civitate Pergami residentes, necnon praefati
Domini Consules qui praecedere debent et debebunt regimini

shown later, the gild judges gradually acquired jurisdiction over all persons actually engaged in trade
within the city, whether members of the gild or not.
As heads of the gild the "consules mercatorum"
administered the law, but the city magistrates were
under a strict obligation, to which they had to swear
on entering upon their office, to aid, if necessary, the
gild consuls with all the powers of the state in
securing the execution of their judicial sentences. In
Italy the Gild Merchant was in fact a subordinate
legislature for commercial purposes. It was not in
every Italian town however that the gild possessed this
important legislative authority. In Genoa for example
the commercial laws are to be sought in the ordinary
civil law of the city. But such cases are rare, and as
a general rule the main body of commercial laws is
in Italian towns contained in the statutes of the
Merchant Gild. The civil codes of the various cities
indeed contained commercial rules of law, but they
merely served to supplement the gild regulations[1].
In commercial matters the consuls decided in the
first place according to the statutes of the gild and
only referred to the common law in cases where the
gild had laid down no rule. Naturally Gild Law
and Common Law occasionally clashed, and the gild

dictae societatis Mercatorum Pergami teneantur, et debeant
executioni mandare omnia et singula statuta et ordinamenta
dictae Societatis ac Communitatis......et si quid actum sit in
contrarium, non valeat nec teneat ipso jure; *et dicta Statuta
habeant et teneant eandem vim, robur et firmitatem quam haberent
ac si facta forent per Consilium Generale Communis Pergami....*"

[1] Lattes, *op. cit.*, p. 71. Lattes' notes 4 and 5 give numerous
references.

statutes sometimes expressly declare that the rule of the gild should be observed, "notwithstanding any statute in the civil law to the contrary[1]."

In the earlier Italian statutes there is little trace of direct borrowing. Their general agreement upon main points is striking, but it was due not to imitation but to the fact that the statutes were everywhere based upon the customs of the merchants, which throughout Italy were much the same. In the 14th and 15th centuries, however, the Lombard towns began to borrow literally or with only slight verbal alterations from one another and, as a natural result, greater uniformity was introduced[2]. This borrowing and slavish imitation was not, as will be seen, confined to Italy, and in other countries it was practised on a far larger scale. In North-Western Europe the customs of one town were often transferred in their entirety, and this system was one of the chief causes that tended to maintain and to increase the general uniformity that characterized the Law Merchant.

The commercial statutes of Italy during the 12th, 13th and 14th centuries will well repay close study. Abounding in detail and regulating every branch of commerce, they provide information upon almost every point of interest. Subject to constant additions and modifications they trace clearly the lines along which commercial jurisprudence was developing: while, framed and fashioned as they were by the merchants themselves, they represent not so much

[1] Lattes, *Il Diritto Commerciale nella Legislazione Statuaria*, p. 75, note 10.

[2] *op. cit.*, p. 61, and notes 24—7.

the law that the State thought best, as the law and customs that were approved by the merchant class. Moreover the early rise and rapid development of commerce in Italy gives a special value to Italian commercial legislation which on many points was in advance of that of other countries. It is in Italy that many of the rules of the Law Merchant had their origin, and it is in Italy that the Law Merchant first developed on a large scale from purely customary to statute law. From every point of view the Italian statutes are of the highest value as sources for the early history of the Law Merchant. Alone however they are altogether insufficient. The Law Merchant varied from country to country, it did not everywhere at the same time pass through the same stage of its development, and the law of every country showed occasional peculiarities that never found general acceptance. Consequently the existence of a commercial rule of law in the early statutes of Italy is no proof of itself that the rule was at that time generally recognised by the Law Merchant throughout Europe.

In Italy, for example, in the Middle Ages it was generally established that the mere possession of a bill containing an alternative clause to bearer—"tibi aut cui hoc scriptum in manu paruerit" or the like —was sufficient to establish a right to payment[1]. It would be hazardous however to conclude that this view was at that time held in all the trading centres

---

[1] Bruschellini, *Trattato dei Titoli al Portatore*, §§ 106 and 107 and note 198: "il portatore di un titolo a clausola alternativa era legittimato ad ottenere la prestazione senza che fosse in verun modo tenuto a dimostrare la legalità del suo possesso." In Southern France, *e.g.* Bearn, the rule held good in the 13th century.

of Europe. As a matter of fact there is good reason
for believing that at that early period mere possession
of such a bill was not everywhere regarded as sufficient
of itself to secure payment[1]. While the Italian
statutes present a fuller and more comprehensive
treatment of early commercial law than is found
elsewhere, they represent after all but one variety of
the Law Merchant, and the laws and customs of the
towns and seaports of France and Spain, England
and Germany need to be examined and compared
before a general view of the development of the early
Law Merchant can be obtained.

In many ways the commercial laws of other
countries were framed and developed under different
conditions from those that prevailed in Italy. For
while in Italy the law of each city was at first mainly
of native growth, showing few signs of direct imitation
of other city codes, in England, France and Germany
the town custumals were broadly speaking based
upon those of a few leading cities. The custumals
of Lubeck, Magdeburg, Cologne, Frankfort and Soest
were transferred to towns in every part of Germany,
while in France Lorris served as a prototype for 300,

---

[1] Des Marez, *Lettres de Foires*, pp. 65—7. The customs of
Malines declare "that no one can exact a debt as bearer of a
letter, if he does not prove that he acts as bearer by procuration
or cession of the person named in the obligation, although the
obligation contains this clause: payable to the bearer of this
letter. "Nyemant en *mach* scult heysschen als bringere des briefs,
tensij dat blijcke dat hi procuratie oft transport heeft van den
ghenen die in de obligatie principalijck genoempt ist, niette-
genstaende dat obligatie inhoudt: te betalene den bringere des
Briefs." Quoted by Des Marez, 67.

Beaumont for more than 500 towns. For its municipal laws Wales went to Hereford, Ireland to Bristol or Breteuil, while Newcastle was one of the principal sources of Scotch burghal law[1]. In Germany the legal tie between parent and daughter city was more closely maintained than in England and France. The court of the German mother city often served as a regular court of appeal from the courts of the cities that had adopted its law. Of these superior courts Lubeck, Magdeburg, Eisenach, Frankfort and Iglau were the most important. Many of the decisions of these courts have been preserved, and in commercial cases their interpretation of the law is the more valuable in that it declares the law not of a single city, but of numerous towns scattered throughout Germany. The reports, for example, of two cases decided in the courts of Magdeburg and Iglau during the 14th century are sufficient to establish for many towns in Bohemia and Eastern Germany the legal effect in bills of an alternative clause to bearer[2]. This system of affiliation of town custumals supplied a unifying force that was in early times absent in Italy. Nor is this the only difference. The merchant gilds had not elsewhere the same direct predominant influence upon the formation of commercial law that the Lombard and Tuscan gilds possessed. Almost everywhere they existed and often they exercised great influence upon the town government, but outside

---

[1] Gross, *Gild Merchant.*

[2] Brunner, *Forschungen*, 655. (Zur Geschichte des Inhaberpapiers in Deutschland.)

Italy their statutes are not so important, considered as sources of commercial law, as the town custumals. Differing largely in bulk and importance from place to place these custumals cannot, with the exception of two or three famous collections of maritime laws, be in any sense considered as commercial codes. Criminal law and administrative details as a rule occupy far more space than purely commercial rules. Still, owing to the lack of other sources, they are often the only authorities available for determining the law that governed commercial transactions within the cities.

The Law Merchant moreover was not everywhere free, as it was to all intents and purposes free in Italy, from the control and influence of external authorities. In England Edward I. changed the law observed in markets and fairs, and in both England and Germany the town custumals required the confirmation of the Lord of the town. Appeals could be made in France from the courts of the great fairs of Champagne to the Parlement of Paris and in England to the Chancellor and Council under the Statute of Staple. Still, though the conditions were not everywhere equally favourable in every country, the town served as a centre for the development of the Law Merchant, for in the towns of every country the essential condition necessary for its development was present. During the 12th and 13th centuries the practical independence of the great commercial cities of Europe was, no doubt, almost unique in Europe, but "everywhere the separation of the town courts from the ordinary courts of the land had been introduced in England and Scandinavia, no less than on the Continent[1]." It was in fair and market and town that the Law Merchant was created and developed, and it is in the records of fair and market, of town and seaport, that the sources for its history mainly lie.

[1] Hegel, *Städte und Gilder der germanischen Völker im Mittelalter*, ii. 506.

CHAPTER III.

THE COURTS OF THE LAW MERCHANT.

IN the 10th and 11th centuries, when the Law
Merchant was in process of formation, the only courts
that could in any sense be regarded as special courts
for commercial purposes were held in markets and
fairs. But as the ·independence of the towns increased and their commerce expanded, there were
gradually created in some of the great cities of
Southern Europe permanent courts distinct from
mere market or fair courts, with a jurisdiction
confined to cases of a commercial character. The
origin of these courts is due to the power, independence and commercial activity of the town; and in
those countries where the central authority was
strong and commerce important, the forces that
created the local commercial court tended to create
courts with commercial jurisdiction for the whole
land. This is however a late development, for it
was but slowly that the central authority became
powerful enough to enforce a uniform system of
judicial organisation, and even when it had the power
it did not always see the necessity of establishing

separate courts of commerce. It was especially for
maritime law that the central power felt the
necessity of special jurisdiction, and in France and
England, for example, the special local courts that
had long existed in seaport and harbour were but
the forerunners of the Admiralty, a national court
with a general jurisdiction in maritime cases. It was
not everywhere that commercial courts arose ; in
most European towns commercial cases were tried in
the ordinary town court, which possessed jurisdiction
in both civil and criminal matters. Apart from purely
maritime courts which are found in many parts of
Europe, it was mainly in Southern Europe where
commercial activity was most intense that special
courts gradually arose with jurisdiction limited to
trade disputes. As in many other branches of
commercial law, Italy led the way.

The rise of commercial courts is in Italy closely
connected with the development of the city constitution. By the end of the 11th century many of
the cities had won practical independence and the
powers of administration and justice had passed into
the hands of their own magistrates. Upon these
magistrates lay the whole burden of the administration of the city republic. In each city their number
was very small and, as in the case of the early
Roman consuls, there was no division of functions :
they were judges as well as administrators. Naturally as the towns grew and commerce expanded the
burden proved too heavy, and during the course of
the 12th century special magistrates[1]—consules

[1] Pertile, *Storia del Diritto Italiano*, II. i. 41, note 49.

judices—were appointed in several towns of Northern Italy. They were not, it is true, in any sense commercial judges, but their creation shows that the old system was inadequate, and partly explains the rapid rise of the aldermen of the merchant gild to importance as commercial judges. For it is only a few years later (1154) that the first notice of the "consules mercatorum" appears; and by the end of the century their existence can be proved in most of the cities of Northern Italy[1]. As heads of the Merchant Gilds these consuls exercised a general control over the members of the gild, which included all or practically all the traders within the town. In addition to political and administrative duties they began to judge commercial cases in which members of the gild were involved, and their court gradually developed from a mere Gild court with jurisdiction only over its own members into a commercial court with jurisdiction over all the cases of a mercantile character that were likely to arise within the city.

In the early gild statutes the jurisdiction of the consuls is limited to the merchants of the city and foreign traders, and the Statutes of Brescia (1313) add the significant definition, "et ille intelligatur mercator qui publice exercet mercathendiam et qui scriptus sit sua spontanea voluntate." Similarly the statutes of Como (1281) give jurisdiction to the consuls over merchants, but add, " merchants are

<hr />

[1] Lattes, *op. cit.*, p. 39, note 1, gives very numerous references. For their general importance see Pertile II. part i. p. 196 and notes.

understood to be those who are or shall be of the merchant gild of Como." It must also be noticed that the jurisdiction of the gild, even over its own members, was not at first of an obligatory character. A member of the gild was within his rights if he summoned a fellow-member before the ordinary civil court of the city instead of submitting the dispute to the decision of the consuls of the gilds. It was however a right that the merchants rarely wished, and still less rarely dared, to exercise. For in the first place legal proceedings were far less expeditious and consequently far more costly in the city than in the gild court. An even more effective reason however was the firm determination of the gild to uphold its jurisdiction over its own members in commercial cases[1]. Under the severest penalties it forbade its members to appeal, in cases where they alone were concerned, to any court save that of the gild. As a last resource the gild did not hesitate to expel members who ignored its claims to jurisdiction, and to forbid trade or intercourse with them. In the same spirit it often compelled foreign merchants as soon as they came to reside in the city to swear to

[1] *Statuto dell' Arte di Calimala dell' anno* 1301 (edited by Filippi), II. c. 38. "Quia facta mercatorum qui inter eos aguntur convenientius tractari possunt coram consulibus artium sub quibus resident litigantes quam coram aliis judicibus, provisum est *quod nulla persona de arte Kallismale possit vel debeat extra curiam consulum Kallismale traere vel convenire aliquam personam que teneatur sub dicta arte Kallismale* in judicio in quo tracteretur vel (word wanting) questio fieret vel moveretur de mercantia mutuo deposito vel cambio vel *alia re ex mercantia descendente* SUB PENA a contrafaciente tollenda ARBITRIO CONSULUM Kallismale."

submit to the jurisdiction of the consuls. Thus, while the jurisdiction of the gild was in theory only concurrent with that of the ordinary civil courts of the city, over its own members and over foreign merchants it was in practice almost exclusive. By the 15th century its claim to exclusive jurisdiction over the commercial transactions of merchants had in many places been acknowledged by the State. At Mantua and Bergamo, for example, the city magistrates were forbidden under the penalty of a heavy fine to interfere in any way with the jurisdiction of the consuls of the gild[1].

Gradually moreover the gild court acquired jurisdiction over non-members. During the course of the 14th and 15th century anyone who carried

---

[1] A.D. 1400. *Lo Statuto dell' Università Maggiore dei Mercanti in Mantova* (edited by Portioli), cap. 41. "Item statuimus...quod *nullus officialis* civitatis Mantuae aut ejus districtus de cetero audeat vel *presumat, aliqualiter, se intromittere de iis quae spectant et pertinent ad jurisdictionem, decisionem,* terminationem et cognitionem *dictorum consulum.* Attenta concessione decretorum et ordinamentorum dictis consulibus indultorum et attributorum *neque ipsorum jurisdictionem quomodolibet impedire....*"

A.D. 1429. *Statute della Mercanzia di Brescia* (edited by Crotta), cap. 44. "Ordinatum est quod D. Potestas Brixiae, praesens et futuri, caeterique officiales nullatenus debeant, sive possint impedire consules Mercantiae Brixiae nec eorum officium, quin possint et valeant juxta statuta in praesenti volumine procedere, et jus unicuique facere, neque possint aliqualiter intromittere de spectantibus et pertinentibus officio praefatorum D. consulum; immo teneantur et debeant, ipsis D. consulibus requirentibus, omne auxilium et favorem pro dicto eorum officio exercendo tam in civitate quam in districtu Brixiae dare et praestare......et quicquid actum fuerit contra praedicta non valeat nec teneat ipso jure...."

on trade, whether member of a gild or not, came to
be regarded from a legal point of view as a merchant
and was subject to the jurisdiction of the consuls.
The gild statutes of Brescia of the year 1313, for
example, only admit the jurisdiction of the consuls
over merchants who had been enrolled as members
of the gild, while the statutes of 1429 add, "etiam
illi qui veniunt vel uti faciant stratas mercantiarum
cum ipsis mercantiis et negotiationibus[1]." At
Florence[2] the city statutes (1415) expressly recognised the competence of the various gild courts
to deal with complaints against non-members,
provided that firstly the defendant did not belong to
any of the other gilds and was a "civis, comitatinus
vel destrictualis florentinus," that is, was a private
citizen, not a merchant, and secondly that the dispute
related to a matter pertaining to one of the gilds.
A few years earlier (1393) they had already secured
legal recognition of their jurisdiction over all those
actually engaged in trade or industry, whether they
were members of the gild or not. At Venice about
the same time there was a dispute between the gild
and the city authorities as to whether the transactions of bankers with their private customers were
under the jurisdiction of the gild consuls; and finally

[1] 1429. St. Merc. of Brescia, cap. 43. In case of doubt as to
the competence of consuls, the consuls and merchants were to
settle the question of competence: "et si quod dubium oriretur,
stetur declarationi praefatorum D. consulum cum quattuor ex
mercatoribus publice utentibus, vel uti facientibus, stratas supra-
scriptas cum mercimoniis vel negotiationibus."

[2] Lastig, *Entwickelungswege und Quellen des Handelsrechts*,
p. 334 and note 2.

the question was settled in favour of the gild.
Everywhere in Italy the jurisdiction of the gild
court was extending, and by the middle of the 15th
century it may fairly be regarded as a special court
for commercial cases[1]. The development however
was not in every town complete; for in some cities
the gild court still retained criminal jurisdiction over
its own members and cannot consequently be considered as a purely commercial court. In many
towns, on the other hand, it was expressly declared
that even when only its own members were concerned
the gild court had merely the right to decide cases
of a commercial nature.

Of Italian commercial courts the Pisan Curia
Maris[2] is especially interesting, as an early example
of a purely maritime tribunal of far earlier date than
the more famous Consulad del Mare of Barcelona,
while its history shows the opposition that the gild
courts experienced from the ordinary courts and the
city magistrates. In the 12th century there were
several courts in Pisa, the most important of which
were the "curia legis" and the "curia usus." The
latter had jurisdiction in commercial and maritime
cases. But just as the gild consuls in other Italian
towns developed into commercial judges, the consuls
of the great Sea Gild of Pisa, the "ordo maris," after
a long and severe struggle obtained sole jurisdiction
and freedom from the control of other courts in all

[1] For the extent of jurisdiction of consular courts see Lattes,
p. 81 and notes 6, 7, 8, and pp. 251—3 with the notes.

[2] For Pisan Sea consulate see Schaube, *Das Consulat des
Meeres in Pisa*, of which I have made great use.

cases of a maritime character. It was only gradually that the city recognised their claims to jurisdiction. In the city statutes of 1233 they were only recognised as "in loco judicum" and were forbidden to decide any cases that came within the Province of the "curia legis." The old jurisdiction of the "curia usus" still remained and was in maritime cases concurrent with that of the sea consuls, whose sentences moreover were still subject to appeal. It would seem that it was only with great difficulty that the maritime court acquired the right of deciding cases finally and irrevocably, for the gild found it necessary to bind its consuls by an oath to do all in their power to procure a law limiting the right of appeal from its court. In a revision of the city laws (1281) their demand was allowed and the right of appeal limited, but it was not till sixty years later that all decisions of the court were recognised by the republic as final and irrevocable. The jurisdiction of the court was extensive, and by the middle of the 14th century covered all cases of a maritime nature. The consuls were entitled[1] to take cognisance of all disputes relating to freights and consignments, and loans and commercial documents connected with maritime trade, and all questions of profits, losses, average and wages, that might arise. Nor are the judicial powers of the consuls less extensive if regarded from the point of view of the persons over whom the consuls were authorised to exercise jurisdiction. That their jurisdiction extended not only over merchants, but also over ship-builders and

---

[1] Schaube, 32—3. Breve ordinis Maris, 2.

carpenters, caulkers, sail, and rope-makers and oakum workers, is not of itself surprising for their connection with the shipping industry is obvious. But the inclusion, among the persons subject to the consular jurisdiction, of joiners, chest-makers, painters, coopers, potters and sadlers, would seem to show that the court was not a purely maritime court. In all probability, however, it would be erroneous to assume that the court exercised jurisdiction over these classes of persons in all cases. Only when they were involved in disputes of a maritime character would they appear before the court of the sea gild. Their inclusion in the list would seem to show that, as in other Italian towns, the competence of the gild court still partly depended upon the profession or trade of the suitors, and that to secure jurisdiction in all cases which were actually of a maritime character the gild found it advisable to procure the insertion of such artisans as joiners, chest-makers and coopers in the list of those who by virtue of their personal occupation were subject to the jurisdiction of the consuls. In the ordinary commercial courts as well as in the maritime courts the test of the Court's competence became gradually less and less a personal test, and the nature of the dispute became more important. But the process was not complete, and at the close of the Middle Ages it was necessary in Italian commercial courts that one at least of the suitors, most often the defendant, must belong by profession to one of the trading or industrial classes regarded as personally subject to the consular jurisdiction. That the personal test had ceased in practice to be of any importance was not so much because the theory had changed as that all classes who were actually engaged in individual or mercantile pursuits were gradually recognised as personally within the jurisdiction of the gild court, and that consequently the occupation or profession of the suitors could rarely be raised as an objection to the exercise of the court's authority.   It should also be noticed that any objection to the competence of the court should in Pisa, as in most other Italian cities, be made at an early stage of the proceeding; and objections made later, even if otherwise valid, are expressly excluded by the statutes[1].   It is interesting to note that the creation of the Pisan "consules maris" and of the English Court of Admiralty was probably due to the same cause.   Schaube has shown for Pisa, and Marsden for England, that the creation of a special jurisdiction for maritime disputes was in all probability due to a desire to keep within due bounds the piratical proclivities of English and Pisan sailors. In England the king was obliged to pay large sums of money as compensation to foreign merchants whose ships had been plundered by English subjects, while at Pisa trade declined and frequent disputes arose for the same reason.

In view of the great importance that the sea consulate acquired in later times, especially in Spain, it seems necessary to lay stress upon the fact that the Pisan court is of earlier date than any similar institution that existed elsewhere.   First mentioned

---

[1] Schaube, 141.

in a document of the year 1201 and probably not in
existence in the preceding year, the Pisan sea consuls
obtained from the State an acknowledgement of their
judicial powers, as early as 1233[1]. For no other
Italian or Spanish city is there satisfactory evidence
that at that date maritime consuls existed with
judicial functions. In Spain the Sea Consulate of
Valencia is the earliest, but it goes back no further
than 1283. Sea consuls are indeed found in Genoa
early in the 13th century (1206), but they possessed
no powers of jurisdiction: they were custom house
officials, not judges, and within a hundred years
their title of sea consuls had changed into the more
appropriate name of "collectors[2]." It was long
thought that earlier instances of the sea consuls
existed in Amalfi and Trani, but the evidence is far
from conclusive. The maritime code of Amalfi, the
Latin redaction of which may possibly date from the
12th century, though the Italian version is as late as
the end of the 14th or the commencement of the
15th century, certainly contains references in both
the Latin and Italian redactions to consuls, but
nowhere are sea consuls mentioned[3]. Schaube
suggests with great probability that the consuls of
the Latin version are the ship consuls that the
merchant vessels of the early Middle Ages often
carried, and that on the other hand it is quite
possible that the consuls of the Italian version
correspond to the sea consuls of Pisa, as they are

[1] Schaube, 4—6 and 14—15.
[2] Schaube, 232.
[3] Schaube, 276. Wagner, *Seerecht*, 62.

often mentioned in the plural and their judicial functions, so far as they are mentioned, are of a maritime character. According to this view, if sea consuls did exist in Amalfi, there is no proof of their existence earlier than the 14th century. To Trani[1] sea consuls have been assigned as early as the middle of the 12th century, for this is the date given for the Trani maritime code in its 16th century Italian translation. The Latin original of the code, however, is not extant, and it is possible that as Pardessus suggests the date 1063 is a mistake for 1363 : Schaube indeed is inclined to place the code as late as the middle of the 15th century. The evidence would seem to show that to Pisa belongs the credit of creating an institution that in the following centuries was to exercise a vast influence upon the development of maritime law in Europe.

The Italian system was not confined to Italy. Trading and settled in every part of Europe the Italian merchants carried as far as possible their institutions with them to their new abode. Accustomed as they were in Italy to be judged in commercial cases not by the civil judges but by the consuls of the merchant gild, they preferred to be judged when abroad by a fellow-merchant according to their own laws. It was one of the most characteristic maxims of the municipal laws of medieval times that the citizens residing abroad should whenever possible seek justice before judges of their

---

[1] Schaube, 277—9. Wagner, *Seerecht*, 61. "Die angegebene Entstehungszeit des (lateinischen) Originals muss aus verschiedenen Gründen bezweifelt werden." Cf. note 3 of Wagner where Sclopis, Capasso and Pertile are cited as accepting the date 1363.

own nationality. Rarely during the Middle Ages would an Italian merchant cite a fellow-citizen before a foreign tribunal; all disputes between citizens of the same Italian town were in foreign cities settled as a general rule by consuls elected by the merchants themselves or appointed direct by the home authorities[1]. "All those," declares a Pisan Law of the 12th century, "who without our bounds are elected captains by the consuls or a public agent, or by the merchants residing there when there is no captain appointed by the consuls or agent, shall be considered "loco judicum." It was by no means necessary that the number of merchants resident in the foreign city should be large. The Placentian statutes (c. 1200), for example, considered three sufficient. These foreign consuls fall into three classes: the "consules missi," the "consules electi" and the "consules hospites." In many great towns, especially those of

. [1] Goldschmidt, 181, n. 143 cites (13th century) out of Statutes of the consules placitorum of Genoa, "Laudabo publice in parlamento quod nullus Janue appellet aliquem vel aliquos Januenses ad extraneum judicem vel extraneam curiam," except "quando Janue consulatus fortasse in ea terra non esset," and gives many other references.

Cf. for Germany Stadtrecht of Soest (1130—1150) cap. 29 in Keutgen, No. 139, p. 141. "Item constitutum est quod si concives nostri extra provinciam inter se dissenserint, non se ad extranea trahant judicia; aut vel inter se litem component, vel, si tot sunt personae, judicem unum de consociis judicem statuant qui litem si potest sopiat: si non potest, causam, donec ad propria redeant, differant. Hoc constitutum, si quis infregerit, x m. et carratam vini vadiabit." The Soest custumal served as model for many other towns. Stadtrecht Münster Bielefeld (c. 1221), cap. 30, Keutgen, p. 152. "Qui suum civem alibi traxerit in judicium, vadiabit ii S."

Eastern Europe, the most important cities, such as
Venice, Genoa and Pisa, had obtained the concession
of one of the town quarters for their merchants.
The importance of these settlements may be judged
from the fact that in the year 1170 no fewer than
20,000 Venetians left Italy upon the Emperor
Manuel's invitation to settle in the cities of the
Byzantine Empire, and that when war broke out
between Venice and the Eastern Empire in the
following year 10,000 Venetians were seized in
Constantinople alone[1]. To administer justice and
exercise a general control in these outlying settlements the Italian city appointed "consules missi."
As officials independent of the local sovereign and
yet exercising jurisdiction over a permanent and
often numerous group of foreign residents, the
consuls naturally seriously limited the power and
authority of the local courts, and they were only
nominated in cases where the Italian city had been
able to persuade the local sovereign by treaty to
waive his full rights of jurisdiction. The consules
electi differed from the consules missi in that they
were elected by the merchants of the colony and as
a rule were to be found in the smaller settlements
and towns of Western Europe, while the consules
missi were only found in large and important
colonies and especially in those situated in the East.
It would seem that in the great fairs of Champagne
the various Italian cities were not only represented
for judicial and administrative purposes by consuls

[1] Giesebrecht, *Die Zeit Kaiser Friedrichs des Rotbarts* I.
pp. 678—9.

of their own, but that all the Italian merchants of Northern Italy formed a union subject to the jurisdiction of the "Capitaneus" or consul of the union. There are numerous references[1] to this official, and that his authority was considerable is shown by the statutes of the Calimala Gild of Florence. For while the special consuls of the Florentine gilds in France had only the right to inflict penalties to the value of 40 shillings, they were instructed to execute the judgments of the "Capitano de' Lombardi," whose power to inflict penalties of unlimited amount is expressly recognised. Outside France however there are no traces of a union of the Italian cities for judicial purposes, and the "Captain of the Lombards" in the Champagne fairs seems to be the only judge recognised in common by the independent cities of Italy during the Middle Ages. In the Italian consular system lies the origin of the commercial consul of modern times; and the consules missi, in particular, form an interesting parallel with the modern European consuls in the Turkish Empire and the far East. Both exercise jurisdiction over their compatriots, both are appointed by the home

---

[1] Goldschmidt, 195—199, Stat. Calimalae (Florence 1301), Lb. iv. rubric 8. "Consules Francie (*i.e.* the Florentine consuls in France) habeant potestatem reddendi jura et cognoscendi de causis usque ad libr. x. turnenses. Item habeant potestatem imponendi usque ad s. xl. cuique et quotiens voluerint pro eorum offitio et ipsam penam auferre. Verum si quod preceptum fecerint alicui de voluntate *consulum societatis lombardorum* tunc possint imponere et tollere penam et penas usque ad libr. 50 *et plus eorum arbitrio.*" In the Italian redaction of the Statutes of 1332, Lb. i. rubric 11, the phrase is "di volontà del capitano de' Lombardi."

government and both owe their judicial powers to a special agreement between the two countries.

The "consul hospes[1]," on the other hand, finds his historical counterpart in the Greek "proxenos." Like the Greek official the "consul hospes" was a citizen of the state in which the merchants under his protection resided, and his tenure of office, like that of the "proxenos," was permanent and not for a limited time as was that of all other Italian consuls. There is however one essential point of difference between the Greek and the medieval official. The "consul hospes" was not only the protector of the merchants of the city which nominated him, he was also their judge, while the "proxenos" of ancient Greece had no judicial powers. "The proxenos," says Schaube, "was the patron of his protégés before all the authorities and before the tribunal; the consul hospes is himself the judge of those who have been recommended to him; the town which nominates him confers upon him the jurisdiction; the town in which he exercises his functions authorises their exercise within its territory in recognition of the principle of personal law and also because the judge depends upon the town itself in his capacity as citizen, and as such is in a relation of close subordination to the local government." In all probability, as Morel has pointed out, the consul hospes furthered in no small measure the adoption by other countries of the principles of Italian commercial law. As citizen of

[1] v. Morel, *Les Juridictions Commerciales au Moyen Age*, 84—88. Schaube, *La proxénie au Moyen Age*. Revue du droit international et de législation comparée, 1896.

the one country and judge of the merchants of the
other he served as a link that connected the legal
system of both.

Almost everywhere the development of commercial tribunals in Italy followed the same line of
progress, and it would seem that in that development
the two main factors were the spirit of liberty and
the identity of the interests of the city with the
interests of commerce. In commerce the Italian
cities of the Middle Ages lived and moved and had
their being. Almost every citizen was an artizan
or merchant and almost every merchant or artizan
was a citizen. The rights and privileges of self-
government in municipal matters taught the citizen
to aspire to self-government in his capacity as
merchant and trained him to exercise those rights
wisely when once they had been granted, while the
identity of the interests of commerce with the
prosperity of the city encouraged the city authorities
to grant a considerable latitude of self-government
and of judicial functions to the merchants and
artisans who formed the mainstay of the State.
Strikingly is the spirit of liberty evident in the free
combination of the merchants in the merchant gild
and in their willing submission to the jurisdiction
of the consuls and their avoidance of the city courts.
Through the loyalty of the merchant to the head of his
gild was slowly evolved the merchant judge, whose
authority the State had finally only to confirm, not
to create.

In the history of the Spanish courts of commerce
the chief point of interest is the rise of maritime

courts of the type of the Pisan sea consulate. In
Spain, the sea consuls were, as in Pisa, maritime
judges with full powers of jurisdiction over all
maritime disputes. At Barcelona there was a curious
reversal of the process of development that took
place at Pisa, where from the "Curia Usus"—a
court with jurisdiction both for maritime and ordinary
commercial disputes—were gradually wrested all
maritime cases, which were transferred to the consulate of the sea. The Barcelona consulate, on the
other hand, originally created as a purely maritime
court, finally developed into a court which took
cognisance of all commercial cases of whatever
nature.

As similar courts of a later date than the Pisan
consulate the Spanish maritime courts naturally
suggest the theory that they were founded in direct
imitation of the Pisan institution. There is much
that supports the theory. It was in the Aragonese
kingdom that the sea consulate in Spain first arose,
and the commercial connection between Aragon and
Pisa was permanent and close. As early as 1233
James I. of Aragon granted trading privileges in the
Balearic Islands to Pisan merchants; and a few years
later (1256) he granted permission to the Pisans in
every part of his kingdom to elect consuls and be
judged according to their own law in all cases, even
those of bloodshed. About the same time (1278)
the Catalonians had their consuls and rectors in
Pisa, and the king of Aragon declared (1284) it was
his intention "always to honour the Pisans as they
have ever been honoured by our predecessors."

Schaube[1], who has gathered and marshalled all
the available evidence, holds that the close commercial connection between Pisa and the Aragonese
kingdom and the striking similarity that existed
between the sea consulate in the two States justifies
the belief that there was in Spain direct imitation
of the Pisan court. On the other hand Goldschmidt,
whose opinion is of the greatest weight, does not
consider the theory proved, though he lays stress
repeatedly on the influence of Pisan upon Spanish
maritime law. The evidence however adduced by
Schaube is so strong that his theory may be regarded
as in the highest degree probable.

It is for Valencia, at the time already part of
the Aragonese kingdom, that there is the earliest
evidence of the existence of a sea consulate. Its
creation (1283) was due to royal charter. Every
year two consuls were to be elected by the "probi
homines maris" and confirmed by the king. Just
as at Pisa the consuls were elected by the sea
gild, they were in Valencia elected by the "good
men of the sea," and in Valencia as in Pisa the
consuls were laymen, skilled "in the art and usage
of the sea." But while in the Italian city the sea
consuls also possessed administrative functions, in
Valencia their powers were solely judicial. The law
that they administered was the customary law of
Barcelona. "They shall decide," runs a clause of
the charter, "contracts and disputes between men
of the sea and merchants, which are to be decided
according to the custom of the sea as it was wont

[1] Schaube, *Das Consulat des Meeres in Pisa*, 239—241.

to be done at Barcelona." In the following year (1284) a judge of appeal was created whose nomination the king reserved to himself. The king however only once exercised his right of nomination, and the election of the judge of appeal lay, as did that of the consuls, in the hands of the "navigators, masters and mariners." The jurisdiction of the court was extensive. "The consuls," declare the regulations of the court (1336—43)[1], "determine all questions which concern freight, damage to cargo laden on board ship, mariners' wages, partnerships in shipbuilding, sales of ships, jettison, commissions entrusted to masters or to mariners, debts contracted by the master who has borrowed money for the wants or necessities of his vessel, promises made by a master to a merchant, or by a merchant to a master, goods found on the open sea or on the beach, the fitting out of ships, galleys, or other vessels, and generally all other contracts which are set forth in the customs of the sea." "The consuls of the sea have all ordinary jurisdiction over all the contracts which have to be determined according to the custom and usage of the sea, and which are declared, stated and specified in the customs of the sea." Perhaps the most interesting feature of the Valencian court was the influence exercised by the mariners and merchants upon the jurisdiction of the court and the law administered by the consuls. This influence was not merely due to the fact that the consuls were themselves merchants or mariners elected in open assembly by the seamen

[1] *Black Book of Admiralty.*

and merchants of the town. In cases where there
were reasonable grounds for suspecting the im-
partiality of the consul or the judge of appeal, the
regulations provided that a prudhomme of the sea
gild should be associated with them, and in the same
spirit the consuls were ordered to take counsel with
the prudhommes of the merchants and of the sea,
should any doubt arise as to what the law on any
point really was. "When one of the consuls, or both,
in any matter are objected to as suspected by either
of the parties who proceed before them and the
reasons of the suspicion are apparent, they have to
associate with them a prudhomme of the gild of
navigators, if one only of the consuls is objected to,
and if both are objected to, they have to associate
with them two prudhommes of the gild of navigators
who are not suspected by the parties.   And together
with these they conduct the proceedings and give
sentence in the matter." "The judge in the same
way, if he is objected to on suspicion, has to associate
with him a prudhomme of the sea gild who is not
suspected by either party." "The sentences which
are given by the said consuls and judge are given
according to the written customs of the sea and in
accordance with what is declared in the different
chapters of them. And there where the customs and
chapters are not sufficient, they give them upon
consultation with the prudhommes of the merchants
and of the sea, that is, always according to the
majority of the voices in council, regard being had
to the persons who give their advice."   It was not
however only in cases of doubt or of suspected

partiality on the part of the consuls that the prudhommes of the sea or merchant gild were consulted.
In every case the opinion of the prudhommes was
taken. If a sentence was to be given "upon a
demand in writing," the "consuls with their scribe
proceed to the prudhommes of the merchants and
cause to be read before them the pleadings and
proceedings in the matters and take thereupon the
advice of the said prudhommes of the merchants.
Afterwards they take counsel of the prudhommes
of the sea…and sometimes they consult the prudhommes of the sea in the first place as it is most
convenient to them. And if the advice of the two
bodies is in accordance, they give sentence in the
matter. And if their advice is not in accordance…
they may confer together; and in case the prudhommes of the sea do not agree with the prudhommes
of the merchants, or will not confer with them, the
consuls may give their sentence according to the
advice of the prudhommes of the sea, for contracts
are to be determined according to the advice of the
latter and not according to the advice of the prudhommes of the merchants, if they do not wish so."
Similarly in cases of appeal the judge takes "counsel
upon the pleadings of the appeal both with the
prudhommes of the merchants and the prudhommes
of the sea; not with those who have given their
advice on the principal pleadings, but with others
in the manner above declared." Evidently maritime
law in Valencia, and probably also in Barcelona from
whence Valencia originally took its law, had by the
middle of the fourteenth century become to a large

extent a written law[1]; but in the interpretation of
that written law and in the judicial recognition of
old usages or new unwritten customs, the judges were
bound to take the advice of the merchants and
seamen of the port, and the influence that seamen
and merchants so exercised upon the development of
the law it is hard to overestimate.

The procedure of the court at first allowed of
long delays, but a royal ordinance of the year 1336
ordering the consuls to administer speedy justice was
shortly followed by "the judicial order of the courts
of the consuls of the sea" which established a
summary procedure similar to that already adopted
in the gild courts of Italy[2]. "The consuls," the
regulation declares, "under charter of our lord the
king have power to hear the plaints and questions
which are brought before them and to determine
them duly, briefly and summarily and forthwith,
without the noise or formality of a judgment, sola
facti veritate attenta, that is to say, looking solely to
the truth of the facts, according as has been accustomed to be done after the usage and custom of the
sea." The summary procedure of the Valencian
court was adopted by the consular courts that later
on arose in other parts of the Aragonese kingdom,
and also by the English Admiralty Courts[3]. The
importance of the regulations of the Valencian court
and the influence they exercised upon the constitution and procedure of late Spanish courts is shown

---

[1] Wagner, *Seerecht*, 57—59.

[2] Schaube, *op. cit.* 245, regulations, c. 36.

[3] *Black Book of Admiralty*. Editor's note.

by the fact that they were placed as an introduction at the commencement of the famous Barcelona code of maritime law and that they were applied to the later consular courts of Spain.

From Valencia the sea consulate of Majorca took its form and constitution, for in the year 1343 Peter the Fourth of Aragon by a charter, the text of which is found in a printed collection of Perpignan charters, authorised the consuls of Majorca[1] to conform to the Valencian "judicial order." In the charter it was expressly stated that "the men of the sea shall assemble every year and elect a consul and judge from among (de) the men of the sea gild who shall determine and decide all cases which arise from maritime transactions." As in Pisa, the jurisdiction of the gild court met with strong opposition. The town government overrode the royal charter and, claiming the right to appoint the consuls and judge of appeal, appointed men who were not connected with maritime pursuits. The king seems to have sided at first with the municipal authorities and to have appointed for life the town clerk as scribe to the consuls. The gild protested and the king gave way, declaring that it was not his intention to act contrary to the charter of 1343.

Only a few years after the institution of the consulate at Majorca a royal charter granted to the sea consuls of Barcelona the rights of jurisdiction that the consuls in the former place possessed. The charter did not create sea consuls at Barcelona, for they existed before and perhaps long before the date

[1] Pardessus, *Collection de Lois Maritimes*, v. 325. Schaube, 246.

when the charter (1347) was granted, though the
earliest certain reference to sea consuls in Barcelona
goes no further than 1302, and it is doubtful whether
they at that time possessed judicial powers.   One
important difference the charter established between
the consulate at Barcelona and the consulate of
Majorca or Valencia.   In the latter the election of
consuls and judge was in the hands of the sea gild,
while at Barcelona their election was entrusted to
the town authorities.   The consuls were however
brought into close touch with the merchants and
seamen of the town by a royal ordinance (1394) which
conferred on the consuls the right[1] to summon
assemblies of the merchants and consuls with them
on matters of commercial interest; at the same time
an elective committee of from ten to twenty
merchants was created and the committee and
consuls were entrusted with administrative functions;
"procurandi manutenendi et defendendi ubique
artem mercantilem." A few years later (1401) a most
important change took place.   The consulate ceased
to be a purely maritime tribunal and was granted by
royal charter jurisdiction in "all civil cases arising out
of mercantile transactions whether by land or by sea."
As in Pisa, it was with difficulty that the Barcelona
court made good its claim to pronounce final
irrevocable sentences; and in 1405, for example, the
freedom of the consulate from the control of royal
courts was seriously endangered.

Appeals were allowed in cases of "restitutio in
integrum," and delay or denial of justice through the

[1] Schaube, 252.

malice or negligence of the judges. Though a serious blow to the power of the consuls, who had urged that in cases that came within their jurisdiction no royal official could in any way interfere, the change was not permanent and a royal charter four years later recognised the claims of the consuls[1].

Gradually the sea consulate was established in the chief commercial towns of Spain, and by the middle of the 17th century it existed in Tortosa, Burgos, Bilbao, Seville and Madrid. Nor was the influence of the establishment of the sea consulate as a recognised institution in the Aragonese kingdom confined to Spain alone. It exercised a great influence in Sicily, Italy and France. At the close of the 13th century, when the royal house of Aragon obtained possession of Sicily and Southern Italy, the consulate, perhaps owing to Pisan influence, was already established in Messina, but under the new dynasty the powers and jurisdiction of the sea consuls at Messina increased[2]. They acquired by the commencement of the 14th century the right to nominate the consuls in foreign cities of all the towns of Sicily and, as at Barcelona, they finally obtained by royal charter (1450) jurisdiction over commercial cases of whatever nature. In all probability this change was due to the influence of the development that the sea consulate had undergone in Aragon. Similarly the political union of Southern Italy with Spain was followed by the almost universal establishment of the sea consulate in the ports of the kingdom of

[1] Pardessus, v. 481—4.
[2] Schaube, 274—5.

Naples. For France Perpignan, the capital of the county of Roussillon, served as the starting point of Spanish influence upon the creation and constitution of the sea consulate[1]. As early as 1388 King John of Aragon "granted to the town of Perpignan the right to have a sea consulate of the form regulated by the charter for Barcelona." " The Perpignan charter," says Pardessus," conferred upon the town the right to establish the consulate and authorised the magistrate to follow the rules relating to competence and procedure traced in the series of 42 articles in use at Valencia." Upon the acquisition of Roussillon by Louis XI. the judicial powers of the sea consuls of Montpelier, who "until then as simple aediles and subordinate administrative officials had been simply charged with the maintenance and super-intendence of the canal and port," were reorganised upon the model of the sea consulate of Perpignan. The royal ordinance (1463) assigned to the consuls maritime cases arising in Montpelier, Argues-Mortes, Agde and the surrounding district and gave them power "de cognoistre des debats, tout ainsi et en la meme forme et maniere que font et ont accoutumé de faire au consulat de mer de la ville de Perpignan." In the course of a century sea consulates were established at Toulouse (1549), Paris (1563) and Marseilles (1565). It would seem that while the sea consulate as a maritime court first arose in Pisa, the diffusion of the institution throughout Southern and Western Europe was due to its general establishment in Aragon and

---

[1] Pardessus, IV. pp. 231, 232, 235.

to the territorial acquisitions and losses of the
Aragonese royal house in Southern Europe.

Long before the introduction of the sea consulate,
by imitation of the Spanish consulate at Perpignan,
commercial courts existed in France[1]. At Marseilles
consuls and judges of appeal for commercial cases
were elected as early as 1162 and their functions
were solely judicial. The consuls at Narbonne, on
the other hand, though elective and possessed of
judicial powers, can hardly be called commercial
judges in the strict sense of the term, as in addition
to important administrative duties they, had jurisdiction in criminal and civil as well as purely
commercial cases. They occupied, in fact, much the
same position as did the Italian town consuls before
the rise of the consules mercatorum as commercial
judges. By some writers the "parloir aux bourgeois[2]"
has been regarded as a commercial court, but its
claim to that title is doubtful. It was the court
of the "Marchands de l'eau" of Paris. To this gild
of merchants Philip Augustus had granted rights of
sovereignty over the course of the Seine. Territorial rights and rights of jurisdiction were inseparable
during the early Middle Ages, and the grant implied
both the power to make regulations for the trade
and navigation of the river, and the power to enforce
those regulations and punish their infraction. To
this duty the "parloir" in the main confined itself,
and of the numerous decisions of the court which
have been preserved the great majority refer to

[1] Morel, *Les Juridictions Commerciales au Moyen Age*, 135—7.
[2] *Op. cit.*, 144—7.

breaches of the privileges of the gild, and it is but very rarely that it determines commercial disputes between individual merchants. It was, as Morel has remarked, only incidentally a commercial court, and its sole importance lies in the fact that as a court composed of judges who were merchants and elected by merchants it may have prepared the way for the creation in the 16th century of the consular judges of Paris, the prototypes of the commercial judges of France from the 16th century to the present time.

Among the commercial tribunals of France the courts of the great fairs of Champagne[1] were until the 15th century the most important. The earliest evidence for the existence of "custodes nundinarum" at these fairs dates from the year 1174. The method of appointment of the guardians of the fair "before the reunion of Champagne and Brie with the French crown is doubtful, but at the commencement of the 14th century they were appointed by the great council of the realm." Originally there were three of these judges, but later the number was reduced to two and finally (1360), as the fairs declined in importance, to one. Though as judges in the greatest fairs of Europe they were mainly occupied in deciding commercial cases, their powers of jurisdiction were not of a purely commercial order. For while on the one hand they had only jurisdiction over merchants and persons frequenting the fairs, and those who wronged merchants on their

[1] Morel, *Les Juridictions Commerciales au Moyen Age*, pp. 148—166. Huvelin, *Droit des Marchés*, 244—258, 390—396, 474—479 etc. Bourquelot, *Études sur les Foires de Champagne*.

way to and from the fairs, on the other hand they possessed so far as these persons were concerned a criminal and unlimited civil jurisdiction. The procedure was summary, and appeal lay in the first instance to the "Grands Jours" of Troyes and finally to the Parliament of Paris. By the close of the Middle Ages the Champagne fair, and consequently the fair courts, had lost all importance and during the course of the 17th century it finally disappeared. At Lyons[1] the fair court developed into a permanent court of commerce. Already in existence in the 14th century the Lyons fair was in 1436 placed for judicial purposes under the authority of the royal seneschal of Lyons, who, as conservator of the fair, "had power, authority and commission to judge and determine without long process or figure of pleading all the disputes which might arise between our said officials and the merchants frequenting the fairs in time of fairs." As in Champagne the nomination of the judge was in the hands of the central authority. Twenty years later the office of "conservator" of the fair was separated from that of seneschal, but the nomination still remained in the hands of the king, and it was not till 1655 after many attempts that the consulate of the town obtained a share in the nomination of the judges of the "conservation." The number of judges was in that year fixed by royal ordinance at eleven: the provost of the merchants and the four echevins were members of the tribunal ex officio; of the remaining six judges two were nominated by the king, four by the consulate

[1] Morel. 166—186. Huvelin, *Droit des Marchés.*

from among the merchants or ex-consuls. During the 16th century the Lyons court ceased to be merely a fair court, and a royal letter of 1602 recognises the jurisdiction of the court "tant en foires que hors foires." The attempts of the merchants of Lyons during the 16th century to secure the creation of elective merchant judges is a characteristic feature of the later development of commercial events in France[1]. Such judges were created by royal ordinance in 1549 at Toulouse and in 1563 at Paris. The Parisian judges had jurisdiction in "tous procès ou différens mûs entre marchands pour fait de marchandise seulement" and were elected in indirect fashion by the merchants. Within a year elective merchant judges were established at Nantes, Bordeaux, Poitiers and Tours. The institution became general and, though modified in points of detail, remains in its broad features unchanged in Modern France.

In Germany[2] commercial courts rose later than in Italy or France. The chief cause of the rise of courts solely for commercial cases was the need of a prompt justice that the civil law of France and Italy, which was based mainly upon Roman Law, did not provide. In Germany however, before the reception of Roman Law, the proceedings were mainly oral and offered little opportunity for long delays[3]. It is probably for this reason that in the inland towns of

[1] Morel, 188—205.
[2] Silberschmidt, *Die Entstehung des deutschen Handelgerichts*, and Morel.
[3] *Op. cit.*, p. 160.

Germany no special commercial courts arose during
the Middle Ages.   But the general reception in
Germany of the Roman Law during the course of
the 14th and 15th centuries made justice less prompt,
and the merchants began to demand the creation of
special courts.   The 15th century saw the rise of
maritime courts in the chief towns of the Baltic.   At
Frankfort the merchants began voluntarily to take
their disputes to a court of arbitration which had all
the characteristics of a commercial court of justice.
There was a definite summary procedure and in
cases of doubt the arbitrators consulted previous
decisions which were carefully recorded and regarded as authoritative in commercial matters[1].   At
Regensburg the merchants seem to have adopted
another expedient to avoid the delays to which the
Roman process gave rise.   During the Middle Ages
the German merchants in their journeys from city
to city were governed and judged by a hanse-reeve.
There is evidence that the Regensburg merchants
possessed such officials as early as the 12th century.
Their name suggests that they were similar to the
Italian gild consuls, but there is a great difference
between the two.   There is no evidence to show
that the hanse-reeve was, like the Italian consul, as
a general rule elected by the merchants[2], and he had
no powers of jurisdiction within his native city[3].

[1] Morel, 107—8.

[2] Morel, 121.

[3] Keutgen, *Urkunden*, p. 198.   Regensburg Stadtrecht, c. 12
(A.D. 1230).   "Item cives potestatem habebunt elegendi haus-
gravium qui disponat et ordinet extra civitatem et non infra ea
tantum que respiciunt negotia nundinarum," cf. Morel, 108.

During the 15th century however the Regensburg hanse-reeve began to exercise jurisdiction in commercial cases within the bounds of the city itself. Repeatedly the schultheiss of the town complains that the inhabitants declare that disputes are of a mercantile character "in order that they may be judged before the hanse court." Von Freyberg includes the court of the hanse-reeve among the Regensburg tribunals and states that it had jurisdiction in commercial cases, of which he especially mentions partnership[1]. As the hanse-reeve was in Regensburg an elective official, his court was of the same pattern as the consular courts of Italy or Marseilles. It was not, however, till the commencement of the 16th century that a commercial court of this type was recognised by the Emperor. In a charter granted to the town of Nuremberg[2] in 1508 the Emperor declared that merchants were the persons best fitted to decide mercantile disputes, and authorised the creation of a number of merchant judges.

The Nuremberg charter however seems, so far as the appointment of merchant judges was concerned, to have been observed for only a short time. But in the following century a commercial court was established (1682) at Leipzig in which the judges were partly laymen and partly jurists, and which served as a model for the later courts of Germany. As in France, the tendency was in favour of lay judges, and in both Germany and France the com-

---

[1] Morel, 109.
[2] Silberschmidt, 59.

mercial courts have retained in their main features
the form and constitution that they assumed during
the 15th and 16th centuries. The commercial
judges of modern France are still merchants elected
for the purpose, and the modern commercial courts of
Germany consist, as did the Leipzig court of 1682,
of merchants and of jurists. Italy alone of the three
countries has broken completely with the traditions
of the past. During the Middle Ages the Italian
commercial judges were merchants who sometimes
had jurists associated with them; from the close of
the Middle Ages down to the 19th century the
system of commercial courts composed not of merchants alone, but of merchants and jurists together,
gradually became the rule and was but the natural
development of the Italian medieval courts. But
the recent abolition in Italy of separate commercial
courts and the transfer of their jurisdiction to the
ordinary courts of common law mark a new de-
parture in the history of the commercial jurisprudence of Italy.

In England as on the continent there were
during the Middle Ages numerous local maritime and
fair courts; and, when for financial purposes the bulk
of the foreign trade of the country was in the 14th
century compelled to pass through a few important
towns, special courts were created in these staple
towns to administer the Law Merchant. A mayor
and two constables were chosen annually to hold the
court of the staple, which had jurisdiction in all
pleas concerning debts, covenant and trespass. As
with the judges were associated two merchants

chosen respectively from among the merchants who
came from the North and those who came from the
South, the court evidently constituted a lay tribunal
similar to the maritime courts of Spain and the
later commercial courts of France.

Appeals lay from the staple courts to the
Chancellor and Council, just as in the contemporary
fair courts of Champagne appeal could be made to
the Parliament of Paris. It would seem that the
association of merchants with the commercial judges
was in England a recognised institution during the
Middle Ages. In the maritime court of Padstow
a case reported for the year 1383 shows that the
trial took place before the mayor and burgesses
assisted by a jury of mariners and merchants[1]. In
fair courts the merchants declared the law. The
records of St Ives Fair (1275) refer to one of the
decisions as "the judgment of the court and of the
merchants"; and a few years later in the same court
a case is respited "until it shall be more thoroughly
discussed by the merchants[2]." The evidence of the
14th century Bristol treatise on this point is most
explicit. "In every 'curia mercati,'" it declares,
"all judgments are to be given by the merchants of
that court and not by the mayor or seneschal. If
the mayor or seneschal should presume to give the
judgments, the person aggrieved should have remedy

---

[1] Marsden, *Select Pleas of Admiralty*, vol. I. Introduction
p. 49.

[2] Maitland, *Select Pleas in Manorial Courts*, p. 187 (1291 A.D.)
and p. 147 (1275 A.D.); *v.* Appendix Nos. 1 and 3.

against them as 'contrary to law and custom and the Law Merchant[1].'"

Fair and Market and Staple courts were all local courts, but during the 14th century the expansion of English trade and the necessity of checking piracy led to the creation of royal maritime courts under the authority of the Admirals of the Fleet. The earliest instance in England of the use of the title of admiral dates from the year 1300 when Gervase Abelard is mentioned as admiral of the fleet of the Cinque ports, but for half a century there is no evidence that an admiral's court existed with judicial powers over non-members of the fleet. In 1357 however there is a reference to a judicial decision of the admiral in a prize case; and three years later a captain of the fleet is appointed with full judicial powers "querelas omnium et singulorum armatae praedictae audiendi et delinquentes incarcerandi castigandi et puniendi et plenam justitiam ac omnia alia et singula quae ad huiusmodi capitaneum et ductorem pertinent et pro bono regimine hominum praedictorum necessaria fuerint faciendi prout de jure et secundum legem maritimam fuerit faciendum[2]." A few months later, upon the appointment of a single

---

[1] Chapter 12, p. 70 in *Little Red Book of Bristol*. The "suitors" of the commercial courts are according to the treatise, c. 12 (p. 71): "omnes illi qui feoffati sunt et residentes infra limites civitatum, feriarum, portuum, burgorum et villarum mercatoriarum, et eciam omnes mercatores qui *ex consuetudine* ferias illas seu mercata visitant, et illi quorum nomina in papiro sunt mercati *nisi* sint clerici vel clericali statu utentes, Comites, Barones, Baroneti, vel milites."

[2] Marsden, *S. Pleas of Admiralty*, Introduction, p. 42.

admiral to command the whole English fleet, a royal
patent was issued authorising the admiral to appoint
a deputy and "giving to him full power...of hearing
plaints of all and singular the matters that touch
the office of the admiral and of taking cognisance
of maritime causes and of doing justice and of
correcting and punishing offences and of imprisoning
and of setting at liberty prisoners who ought to
be set at liberty, and of doing all other things that
appertain to the office of admiral as they ought to
be done of right and according to the law maritime[1].
The jurisdiction of the Court of Admiralty as
established by the admiral's patent was vague and
gave the court full scope to extend its power.
Complaints were made by the local courts of the
encroachments of the Court upon their jurisdiction.
"Because," declares a statute[2] of 1390, "great and
common clamour and plaint have often been made
before this time and still are made that the admirals
and their deputies hold their sessions in divers
places within the realm, both within franchise and
without, taking to themselves greater power than
belongs to their office, to the prejudice of our Lord
the king and of the common law of the realm and to
the great damage of divers franchises, it is granted
that the admirals and their deputies shall not in
future meddle with anything done within the
kingdom, but only with anything done upon the sea
as was the custom in the time of the noble King
Edward III." This act does not seem to have been

[1] Marsden, S. Pleas of Admiralty, Introduction, p. 43.
[2] Black Book of Admiralty, I. 412.

found sufficient to restrain the encroachments of the admiralty, for two years later the limits of its jurisdiction were more carefully defined. "It is declared, ordained and determined," runs the statute, " that of all contracts pleas and plaints and of all other things done and arising within the body of counties as well by water as by land and also of wreck of the sea, the court of the admiral shall have no cognisance, power or jurisdiction; but that all such contracts, pleas and plaints and all other things rising within the bodies of counties as well by land as by sea as aforesaid and also wreck of the sea shall be tried, determined and discussed and remedied by the laws of the land and not before the admiral nor his lieutenant in any way: nevertheless of the death of a man and of a mayhem done in great ships being and hovering in the main stream of great rivers, only beneath the bridges of the same rivers near the sea and in no other places of the same rivers the admiral shall have cognisance[1]." Shortly after the accession of Henry IV. a remedy was provided for those who had been sued, contrary to the terms of the statute of Richard II., in the Court of Admiralty, enabling them to recover double damages in the ordinary courts from the plaintiff, who was moreover liable to a fine of £10. The common law courts issued frequent writs of prohibition based upon the statute of 1392 and checked encroachments on the part of the admiral's jurisdiction. At first the admiralty adopted the system of trial by jury, which was still in vogue

---

[1] *Black Book of Admiralty*, i. 413, 414.

in the middle of the 15th century[1]. By the middle
of the 16th century however the jury system had
been replaced by trial by witnesses. The procedure
and the law administered were largely based upon
the Roman civil law. The towns of Bristol, Bridg-
water, Exeter, Barnstaple and Wells complain as
early as the reign of Richard II. " of the delays of
the law civil," and in the 15th century "articles of
the lieutenant general of the high admiral " it was
provided that the judges " should only mix the law
civil with the law maritime there where it may
be equitable." The activity of the court increased
under the Tudors, but during the 17th century a
determined attack was made upon its jurisdiction
by the common law courts. The attack was in the
main successful, and most of the civil jurisdiction
of the Admiralty courts was usurped by the courts
of common law, and not recovered till the 19th
century.

It was not only at the expense of the Admiralty
that the common law courts extended their jurisdiction. During the 15th century the merchant
gilds in England lost much of their importance ;
and though a few fair courts still continued and the
courts of some of the larger cities retained their
jurisdiction, the common law courts began to occupy
themselves with commercial cases of every kind.
During the 17th century the decisions of Lord Holt
and Lord Mansfield introduced into English common
law most of the customs and usages of English

[1] Marsden, *S. P. of A.*, Introduction, 54. *Black Book of
Admiralty*, vol. I. p. 267.

merchants, and the Law Merchant became an integral part of the common law of the realm, and the common law courts practically the only courts where commercial cases were decided. While France and Germany still adhere to the medieval system of separate commercial courts entirely or partly composed of lay judges, England had by the 17th century already begun to transfer the jurisdiction over commercial cases to the ordinary law courts, and by the 18th century the process was practically complete. But to the local commercial courts of the Middle Ages and to their merchant judges Western Europe owes a great debt. Out of their own needs the medieval merchants created their own courts and in those courts evolved, expanded and systematized a body of commercial law, speedy, equitable and flexible, which forms the basis of the commercial rules of modern times.

CHAPTER IV.

PERSONS.

THE merchant was during the two or three centuries that followed the rise of the Law Merchant almost invariably a member of a gild which early acquired a monopoly of trade for its members. In England such clauses as "We grant a gild merchant with a hanse and other customs belonging to the gild so that no one who is not of the gild may merchandise in the said town except with the consent of the burgesses" are found in practically all the Merchant gild charters from the 13th century onward. Though in most of the countries of the continent the gild did not exercise the influence upon the government of the town that it often exercised in England, nearly everywhere the gild existed and secured for its members, in early times at any rate, a practical monopoly of trade. It would be wrong indeed to assert that even during the early period of the gild system all who were actually engaged in trade belonged without exception to a gild, but for long such cases were the exception and not the rule. The general insecurity and lawlessness that characterised

the early centuries of the Middle Ages forced the
medieval merchant to organise and to combine in
order to defend his own interests. But though the
gild was perhaps at first a necessary expedient in a
lawless age, it proved, with its tendency towards
exclusiveness and its narrow-minded desire to develop
not so much the trade of the whole country as the
trade of its own locality, a hindrance rather than a
help to the development of commerce as order was
gradually established and nations and kingdoms
gradually rose out of feudal anarchy. When towards
the close of the Middle Ages France and Spain,
Sicily and England, Denmark and Scandinavia
formed well organised kingdoms, a commercial
system that regarded the merchant of one city as an
alien when trading in another city of the same
kingdom no longer corresponded to the needs of the
time. Commerce had outgrown the period of
municipal exclusiveness that the gild system represented, and the gild everywhere lost much of its
power and importance. Gradually the merchant was
freed from the necessity of joining the gild and
the development of commerce was left to individual
initiative and enterprise. The gild however proved
to be long lived, and centuries after it had outlived
its day of usefulness it continued in some countries
to enforce rules and regulations no longer adapted
to the new political and economic conditions of
Europe.

In Italy the emancipation of the individual
merchant from the monopoly of the gild began
early; for in commercial development it was far in

advance of other countries and it realised earlier than was realised in most countries the evils of absolutely confining trade and commerce to a close corporation. As elsewhere, the privilege of trading and manufacturing was at first confined, with rare exceptions, to members of the various gilds, and the old rule was maintained in many places until the close of the Middle Ages and even later[1]. As early as the 13th century however some of the town statutes freed both merchant and citizen from the obligation of entering a gild; and the frequent employment in the statutes of such expressions as "consueti," "usitati," "usevoli mercatores" shows that in Italy there existed during the 14th and 15th centuries a well recognised class of merchants who were not members of the gild[2]. The same change, though generally later than in Italy, took place elsewhere, and slowly it became no longer necessary for the trader to be a member of a gild to enjoy the legal privileges of a merchant. Foremost among those privileges was the right to be judged by the Law Merchant. That law was in its origin a personal law, the law of a special class. In virtue of his profession the merchant had a right to be judged by a law different from the common law. It was a law based largely upon the usages and customs of the merchant class and often administered by the merchants themselves. The Law Merchant in the main retained throughout the Middle Ages this characteristic feature. In England the view that

[1] Lattes, p. 82, note 1. Pertile, vol. II. part i. p. 180.
[2] Lattes, p. 81 and notes.

the application of the principles of the Law Merchant
was a legal privilege, to which the merchant alone
could lay claim, was maintained in part till the end
of the 17th century. In 1613 the plea that an
acceptor of a bill of exchange was not a merchant
was held by the court to be a good defence to a
claim on the bill, and it was not till 1692 that the
English courts ventured to ignore the personal
character of the Law Merchant by deciding that if
gentlemen accepted bills they ought to pay them[1].
France had effected the same development a century
earlier, and the Paris court of commerce, which was
established in 1563, and the numerous courts of
which it was the model, had jurisdiction and applied
the Law Merchant in all cases of bills of exchange
whether the parties to the suit were merchants or
not. The main course in the development of the
legal status of the merchant would seem to be that
this status, long confined to members of a close
corporation, was gradually extended to all those
actually engaged in trade, and that the merchant
gradually ceased to have an exclusive claim to
the speedy and practical justice of the Law
Merchant.

In countries where the Roman Law prevailed
the Law Merchant does not seem in early times to
have been able to secure freedom of contract for the
married woman. In Italy, for example, she could
only carry on business with the consent, express or
tacit, of her husband, who was responsible in virtue
of that consent for the execution of all contracts

---

[1] Sarsfield *v.* Witherby, Carthew 82, quoted by Scrutton, p. 30.

that she might make[1]. In the case of "filii familias,"
however, the influence of German law and the
necessities of commerce triumphed over the maxims
of Roman law even in Italy, where the common law
of the land was in the main Roman, and a filius
familias actually engaged in trade on his own
account was considered "sui juris" even though he
continued to live in his father's house[2].

The agents and factors of the merchant were
in Italy subject like the merchant himself to the
jurisdiction of the commercial courts and they could
claim to be judged according to the Law Merchant in
commercial disputes with one another or with their
master. In case of their employer's failure they
were in many Italian towns held liable, under
certain circumstances, for his debts, and they had
the right to conclude contracts binding upon the
merchant whose factor they were[3]. Consequently
the distinction between factor and partner was often
of no great practical importance; and in a letter sent
from Pisa to Florence in 1310 it was declared that
in mercantile usage "factor" and "socius" had the
same significance[4].

In England however as late as the reign of
Edward I. the whole common "law of agency was
still in its infancy." But whatever view the king's
courts might take, the Law Merchant in England
recognised in the 13th century that when an agent

---

[1] Pertile, III. pp. 309, 310.
[2] Pertile, vol. III. p. 380, n. 32.
[3] Lattes, p. 103, notes 11 and 14. Goldschmidt, pp. 249, 250.
[4] Goldschmidt, 250, n. 51.

bought goods the property was vested in the principal not in the agent. A case in the fair court of St Ives for the year 1291 illustrates this point. Hugo Pope was distrained in a suit by means of a horse. "And thereupon a certain Alan of Berkhamstead comes—and alleged in full court that the said horse was his and that he had bought the horse for his own for use of a certain Thomas of 'Rammesden,' and he placed himself of his own free will on the inquest, and the opposite party likewise. And the inquest—comes and says that the said Alan unjustly claims the horse as his own; nor has he any part in the horse because the said Alan bought the horse to the use of the aforesaid Hugo as the 'valet' and broker of Hugo; and Hugo instructed him to pay 20 shillings in the name of Hugo for the horse—wherefore it was considered that the horse be kept and taken until the aforesaid Hugo shall have given satisfaction[1]."

The Bristol Treatise on the Lex Mercatoria gives a valuable account of the legal relations of master and servant in their bearing upon transactions with third parties. "Because frequently and generally it happens," the treatise declares, "that apprentices and 'sub-merchants' who publicly and openly trade under their masters procure the loan and accommodation of money, goods and merchandise to their masters' use, and if they were borrowing by themselves and not for masters of this kind, one would not deliver to them goods at all,—it is ordained that the masters of these apprentices and sub-merchants shall in the same way be answerable

[1] See Appendix No. 4.

for goods and merchandise delivered to them in any
way by the hands of their apprentices and sub-
merchants just as if they themselves had received
those goods and merchandise with their own hands,
provided that the apprentices and agents (submer-
catores) are known to be under their master and to
be openly serving and trading with the goods of
their master before and after an exchange or
delivery of this kind, or at any rate at the time of
such exchange and delivery. Moreover if their
property has been advanced, handed over or in
any way delivered by their agents or other of their
men, the merchants have the same action against all
persons in suing for their goods and merchandise as
if they themselves had advanced, delivered or
handed over the goods and merchandise[1]." The
Law Merchant in England recognised the responsibility of the principal for the acts of his agent
provided that the agency was open and well known,
and based that responsibility upon the equitable
grounds that credit was generally given to the agent
simply because it was believed that he was acting
on behalf of his master.

If the merchant enjoyed many privileges in his
own country and elsewhere, as a foreigner he was
subject when abroad to many legal disabilities, which
were partly a survival from primitive times when
the stranger in a foreign land was a rightless person
unprotected by the law. Defenceless as he was the
foreign merchant in olden times obtained a security
that the law did not give by placing himself under

[1] Chapter VII. *Little Red Book of Bristol*, p. 66.

the protection of a powerful individual able and willing to protect him. It was even in historical times often a very necessary precaution. "The Saxons sold the stranger who had no patron[1]." Gradually the head of the State took the foreign merchant under his special protection, but the stranger had to pay the price. Not only was he often subject to dues and tolls that the native merchants did not pay, but if he died intestate and without children the king, and where feudalism triumphed the local authorities, laid claim to any of his property that happened to be within their jurisdiction. It would seem that during the 12th and 13th centuries this right of "aubaine" became more oppressive. Originally the stranger had a right to make a will, and if he had children they succeeded to his possessions, but the feudal lord and the free commune, and in France the king himself, overrode both testament and rights of the stranger's children[2].

It is to the credit of the Papacy and the Church that it used its vast influence to remedy this injustice; and as early as the middle of the 12th century (1109) the Pope abolished the "jus Albanagii" within the papal States. The influence of the Church was not exerted in vain, and Frederick II. (1220) forbade the exercise of the right within the bounds of his Empire[3].

[1] Meginardi, *Translat. S. Vitti*, c. 13, "Peregrinum qui patronem non habebat vendebant Saxones." Quoted by Pertile, III. 187, n. 1.

[2] Pertile, III. 194. Viollet, *Histoire de Droit...*p. 368. For the right of aubaine in general see Caillemer, *Confiscation et administration des successions*, 147, 178.

[3] Schroeder, *Deutsche Rechtsgeschichte*, p. 530, note 52.

But the decline of the imperial power in Italy led in that country to a revival of the custom, while in France the financial necessities of the crown increased the severity of the law. Not only were the children of the alien debarred from their father's inheritance, but a new maxim—"aubains ne peuvent succéder"—was added to the old adage "aubains ne peuvent tester." But the custom ran counter to the true interests of commerce. The law itself the merchant was unable during the Middle Ages to abolish, but the great mercantile cities and countries by special treaties procured exemption from the law for their citizens, the richer merchants effected the same purposes by obtaining letters of naturalisation, and the greater fairs were gradually freed, in France if not elsewhere, from the operation of the law. In 1364, for example, all the Castilian merchants trading in France were exempted from the right of aubaine; and in 1340 a merchant in return for hard cash obtained recognition of the right of his children to inherit, and of his own right of testation "tout aussi bien comme sil fust nez franchement de nostre royaume; et voulons que pour cette cause il ne doie, ne puisse jamais estre reputez pour aubaine, epave, ou etrange de nostre royaume." As early as 1294 a treaty concluded between the captain of the Lombards frequenting the fairs of Champagne, and the Count of Salins, established that "if any of these merchants die within our land or jurisdiction, or their messenger or servant, we will cause his goods to be consigned and rendered to his messenger or partner—or to the messenger of the union of the

said merchants or of the captain, as soon as they
have been demanded from us or our bailiff; but he
who has received the goods shall carry the will of
the deceased. " The privilege was extended to a great
number of fairs[1]. A 15th century ordinance (1465)
of the fair of Chalon-sur-Saône granted permission
" to all the said foreign merchants to make wills and
provide for the disposal of their property according
to their good pleasure. And in case the said foreign
merchants should die in our land intestate, those who
ought to inherit according to the written law, the
statutes or customs of the country, inherit fully and
without opposition, as if they had died in the place
of their nativity or where they abode. " But in spite
of numerous exemptions the old disability still continued to be recognised by the law and was not
abolished in Savoy till 1633 and in France till the
French Revolution[2].

The exercise of the right of aubaine was greatly
limited during the course of the Middle Ages by the
rise of national kingdoms and the increase of the
power of the crown throughout the greater part of
Europe. The feudal lord had been inclined to regard
the mere stranger to the locality as subject to the
right of aubaine even though he might be a citizen
of the country, while the king only exercised the
right over strangers to the realm.

The aliens however were subject to restrictions
of a more purely commercial character than was the
right of aubaine. The usage of commercial towns

---

[1] Huvelin, *Droit des Marchés*, pp. 444, 445.
[2] Pertile, iii. pp. 197, 198 and notes 47 and 54.

in medieval Europe confined the trade of foreign
merchants within the narrowest limits. As a
general rule they were not allowed, except in fairs
and in some towns on certain market days, to buy
from or sell to other strangers, and retail trade was
very often absolutely forbidden. During their stay
they were to lodge with a "host" appointed by the
town or gild magistrates, and the host was held
responsible for the behaviour of his guests and
expected to see that they did not infringe the rights
of the citizen by retail trade or by dealing with other
strangers. On the whole these restrictions were
maintained till the end of the Middle Ages. In
England indeed the foreign merchant, to the great
discontent of the towns, was freed during great part
of the reigns of Edward III. and Richard II. from
these restrictions, but under the Lancastrian kings
they were once more reimposed. The rule that the
foreign merchant should "go to host" seems in
England to have fallen into disuse in the 15th
century, but that it was maintained on the continent
is shown by the bitter complaint of a pamphleteer
that the foreigner fared better in England than the
English abroad.

> "What reason is't that we should go to host
> In their countries, and in this English Coast
> They should not so ; but have more liberty
> Than we ourselves[1]. "

To this desire to limit and control the operations
of foreign merchants in the interests of the locality

---

[1] Quoted in Ashley, *Economic History*, vol. I. part ii. p. 17.

is partly due the important position that the brokers[1] gradually acquired. In the Roman Empire brokers already existed but, unorganised and uncontrolled by the laws, they occupied a far less important position than fell to their lot during the Middle Ages. Ulpian calls their occupation sordid, and Horace describes the merchant who had failed to succeed when trading on his own account as a last resource turning broker. In the Middle Ages however brokers had almost attained on the continent to the rank of public officials. They were as a rule limited in number, appointed by the gild or city magistrates, and required to be of good repute and citizens of the town. At times the regulations plainly show that the brokers were appointed in the interests of the local monopoly. "We appoint," declares a decree[2] of the town council of Vienna of the year 1348, "for the merchant and traders six brokers who are landowners, and true and honest folk who shall go into their bargains, and they and no one else shall truly serve strangers and citizens ......and every broker, when he learns that a stranger is travelling through the land against the right of the town and the gild, shall bring the matter before

[1] For the position of brokers in Medieval Italy see Rezzara, *Dei Mediatori e del Contratto di Mediazione*, in which numerous and long quotations are given from various city statutes of Italy.

[2] Keutgen, *Urkunden*, No. 236, p. 330. St. Calimalae (Florence 1301), Lb. v. cap. 1, p. 157, "Item jurent *sensales denumptiare secrete consulibus* Kallismale omnes et singulos mercatores facientes contra formam capituli constituti hujus vel contra ordinamenta loquentia de sicuritate averis Kallismale et hominum dicte artis et de *retinentibus hospitum forensium et de scribentibus et promictentibus pro forensibus et de ipsis forensibus......*"

the gild reeve as he has sworn to do. " It was
everywhere their duty to keep a written account of
the transactions which had been arranged by their
mediation. At Cologne[1] (c. 1400) " to avoid all
quarrels and disputes which might arise between
merchants with regard to money or sales, the hosts
and brokers were to swear to write down every sale."
In the Italian statutes the duties and legal privileges
are treated with unusual detail, and their position as
public officials is recognised by the law courts. In
disputed cases the courts admitted the principle that
the evidence of the broker's books was to be regarded
as correct unless there was definite proof of the
contrary.

The 13th century gild statutes of Piacenza
declare "that if a dispute arise about contracts or the
price of goods, the broker who arranged the bargain
shall be believed on his simple word," while the
statutes of Cremona[2] (1388) which contain a similar
regulation show with what care the books were
required to be kept. " The brokers are bound to
write with their own hand, or to have written, all the
sales which they make of the value of 25 imperial
pounds or above, if complete payment has not been
made, in a book, which shall be kept at the office of
the gild with the consuls and shall be bought with
the money of the gild, declaring the name and sur-
name of the buyer and seller, the article sold and
its price and the date fixed for payment; and this
they are bound to do within eight days of the day

[1] Keutgen, *Urkunden*, No. 237, cap. 12, p. 331.
[2] Quoted by Rezzara in *Dei Mediatori*, p. 53.

that the bargain was made......and the book placed
in the office of the gild shall be believed unless
there is proof to the contrary." To secure im-
partiality it was a general rule that no merchant or
partner of a merchant should be a broker, and that
if he had a personal interest in any transaction he
should inform the parties. Occasionally the statutes
go further and absolutely forbid the broker to
negotiate the sale of any goods in which he is in
any way interested. Appointed as he was by the
authorities, authorised to report the misdeeds of
foreigners and to keep a record of their sales and
contracts, in which his mediation was often declared
necessary by the laws, and possessed of a legal claim
to be believed in virtue of his office[1], the medieval
broker occupied on the continent a position of public
trust and authority which he did not possess in the
Roman Empire and which he no longer retains in
modern times.

[1] St. of Bergamo 14, cap. 57. "Mesetti (*i.e.* brokers) teneantur
in scriptis dare quodlibet mercatum...et tali mercato in scriptis
producto credatur et plena fides adhibeatur." St. of Brescia,
cap. 9, same expressions verbatim.

CHAPTER V.

SALES AND CONTRACTS.

In sales neither Roman nor Germanic law satisfied the requirements of the medieval merchant, and very early traders began to assert maxims of their own better suited to their needs. It was in market and fair that in all probability the new rules first became customs that ripened into laws. Early in the 11th century a German poet writes that merchants were asserting the validity of sales made in fairs, though concluded without the usual formalities. That the merchants should try to alter the existing law regulating sale and possession of goods is not surprising. Neither Roman nor Germanic law gave to the bargains of merchants that security and certainty that the interests of commerce demanded. Neither protected against the claims of the original owner the merchant who had in perfect good faith bought goods stolen or lost, and neither secured the validity of a sale confirmed by an earnest. According to Roman law the rights of the original owner remained good against all third parties whether they had acquired possession in good faith or not, and whether the goods had been stolen from the owner himself or from a person to whom he had entrusted them.

The laws of the Teutonic nations, however, only recognised the right of the original owner of stolen property to make good his claim against third parties, if it was actually in his own possession when it had been lost or stolen. If he had lent or entrusted the article to any one from whom it was afterwards stolen, he had only a right of action against the person to whom it had been confided[1].

But this did not make the position of the bona fide purchaser more secure; for though the original owner had lost all right of action against third parties, that right had merely passed to the person to whom the goods had been entrusted. A merchant was at any time liable to be called upon to defend his right to goods that he had purchased, if they should prove to be stolen or lost property. If he could not name the person from whom he had bought them, he not only lost his property but ran the risk

---

[1] Schroeder, p. 273.

Pertile, IV. 256 and notes 26 and 27.

Sachsenspiegel II. 61, § 1. "Welcher Mann...fahrende Habe dem anderen leiht oder versetzt, verkauft sie dieser, wird sie ihm gestohlen oder geraubt; jener mag darum keine Foderung haben, als gegen den dem er sie lieh oder versetzte."

Brunner, *Rechtsgeschichte*, II. 509. "Wurde die Sache nicht dem Eigentümer, sondern einer treuen Hand gestohlen, in der er sie gelegt hatte, so war nur diese in der Lage, den 'Anefang' durchzuführen und die Diebstahlsbusse in Anspruch zu nehmen."

Friese und Liesegang, *Magdeburger Schöffensprüche*, Nos. 1, 1. III. A 45, pp. 4, 418, 709, 710.

Maitland, *History of E. L.* II. 163—6.

of being punished as a thief. Even if he was in a
position to produce the seller, he did not retain the
goods, and the vouchee whom he had produced was
called upon to explain how the goods had come into
his possession. He could defend himself in the same
way by producing as warrant the person from whom
he had made the purchase, and it would seem that
the process could at first be continued indefinitely.
Gradually, however, the process came almost everywhere to be regarded as complete when the third
warrant appeared before the Court[1].

That in the 13th century English merchants
were attempting to secure protection in the possession
of stolen goods bought in market and fair, and that
their claim was not recognised by the king's courts,
is apparent from the evidence of the legal writers of
the time. "If the accused," writes Britton[2], "has any
warrant within our realm, then he may defend
himself by voucher, and if he vouched to warrant any
person who gave him the thing, or sold it or otherwise
made it over to him, let a day be given him to
produce his warrant if he be not present.......If the
vouchee comes and enters into the warranty to
defend the voucher in the possession of the thing, let
the plea against the principal be suspended and one
commenced against the warrant. And if the warrant

---

[1] Brunner II. 503 and notes 51—5. Brunner quotes Otto I.'s
legislation, "Tunc tercius warens juret quod nec latro fuit, nec
collega latronis, sed cum suo proprio pretio comparavit et *reddat
rem*," and refers to Canute II. 24 § 2, William I. 45, Leges Henrici
primi c. 64, § 6. Cf. Pertile IV. 252 note 13; cf. however case (c. 1500)
cited above, p. 94, note, *Magdeburger Schöffensprüche*, III A 45.

[2] Britton, edited by Nichols, I. 57—60.

makes good his case then let both the voucher and his warrant be acquitted and the plaintiff sent to prison.......If the judgment be given against the warrant, then the thing challenged shall be adjudged to the plaintiff and the principal shall be indicted of felony at our suit, upon presumption of his being an accomplice of the warrant who is attainted of the felony. If the principal has no one to vouch, he may say that he bought the thing at such a fair or such a market in the presence of a great number of people, and paid a toll to the bailiffs for it. And if he vouches the testimony of the said bailiffs and other then present and evidence is given accordingly, or if he put himself on the country and is acquitted of the felony, and yet the prosecutor has proved that the thing challenged belonged to him and that it was stolen from him or out of his custody, in such case he must be answerable to the owner and give him satisfaction, and judgment shall be that the claimant recover the thing challenged and that the person challenged go quit and lose what he gave for the thing; and if he can produce no such witnesses let him acquit himself by the country." Evidently merchants were beginning to urge that a distinction should be drawn between stolen goods bought in market and fair and those bought elsewhere. The evidence of Bracton is equally strong. "If a person should buy a stolen article, though he believe it to be legally purchasable, then if he cannot produce a warrantor, a distinction must be made whether he has bought it publicly in a fair or in a market, and in the presence of the bailiffs and other honest men who might give testimony of the fact and that he paid toll and customs; such a purchaser shall be set free when he has returned the article to the true owner; but nothing shall be returned to him of the price which he paid; but if he have none of these defences he will be in peril[1]."

As late as the 13th century "stolen goods can be recovered by legal action not only from the hands of the thief, but from the hands of the third, the fourth, the twentieth possessor, even though those hands are clean and there has been a purchase in open market[2]." Evidently the law hampered sale and barter. "Commercial business cannot be carried on if we have to inquire into the title of everybody who comes to us with documents of title such as bills of lading or for the sale of goods[3]."

The financial necessities of the Lords of market and fair, and the increasing importance that was attached partly under the influence of the Church to the element of good faith, contributed to the triumph of the principles asserted by the merchant classes. Fairs and markets were most valuable sources of revenue to the feudal lord, who was not slow in seeing that to protect the honest purchaser in the possession of his goods was likely to increase the importance and consequently the revenue of his fair. Gradually sales in market and fair were specially protected. The merchant who had purchased in good faith was either allowed to keep possession of the goods or at the worst only bound to return

---

[1] Bracton, Fol. 151.   [2] Pollock and Maitland, ɪɪ. 165.
[3] Scrutton, *Mercantile Law*, p. 23.

them if the original owner was willing to refund the
price that had been paid for them.   But if the thing
shall have been sold, declares the fair charter of
Chapelande[1] for the year 1075, and the buyer has
lawfully proved that he was unaware that it was a
thief from whom he bought it......(the owner) shall
have his property and pay the buyer what he gave
for it. Beaumanoir writing in the 13th century
gives the same rule. "But if he, who has the thing,
has bought it in common market, he, who is claiming
his property which he has lost or which was stolen
from him, shall not have it back, if he does not
refund the money which the buyer paid for it[2]."   In
Italy the statutes of Nice established that anyone
who bought anything openly and in good faith
"shall not be bound to return it to its owner, unless
he restore to the buyer the price which he had paid."
By the 14th century the principle that purchase in
open market gave sure possession in stolen goods, or
entitled the purchaser to claim the price, was gaining
ground in France, Germany and Italy[3], and a case

[1] Huvelin, *Droit des Marchés et des Foires*, p. 455.

[2] Beaumanoir, cited by Pertile iv. 258, note 35. " Se chil qui
a la chose l'acheta al marchié quemun, chil qui poursuit sa
chose—qu'il perdit ou qui li fu emblé, ne la raura pas se il ne
rend l'argent que l'acheterres en paia. Mais si il l'avoit achetée
hors de marchié par mendre pris que la chose ne vauroit—et il ne
pouvoit trouver son garant, li demandierres raauroit la chose
sans l'argent de la vente paier."

[3] Pertile, iv. p. 258 and numerous quotations and references in
note 35.

Goldschmidt, p. 299 note 3.

Schroeder, *Deutsche Rechtsgeschichte*, p. 711 and note 11.

Heusler, *Deutsches Privatrecht*, ii. p. 215. " Wichtiger ist tried in the fair court of St Ives for the year 1291 would seem to show that, though not yet adopted by the courts of common law, the principle of bona fide possession had already become part of the Law Merchant in England. A certain Alice complains of Mathilda Frances "about three bushels of malt found in the hands of the said Mathilda." The plaintiff was obliged to find surety that she would prosecute the case. But when the case came before the court she refused to pursue the plea, and she and her pledges were punished and the case was not allowed to drop. "Thereupon," continues the roll, " the seneschal ex officio, as though on the suit of the king, demanded of the said Mathilda Frances in whose seisin the malt has been found, how she wished to defend herself (from the charge) that the malt had not been acquired by theft. And she says that for good and for ill she placed herself on God, and the sworn neighbours; who come and say on their oath that a certain stranger whom Mathilda herself did not know had brought the malt to her house, and that upon the malt Mathilda had given him in exchange eight pence, and that she did not suspect the stranger of any theft. And therefore it is considered that the said Mathilda together with her malt be quit[1]."

die Neuerung zu Gunsten des gutgläubigen Erwerbers. Sie besteht darin dass wer eine gestohlene Sache auf offenem Markte gekauft hat, gegen die Klage des Bestohlenen geschützt wird."

Jobbé-Duval, *Revindication des Meubles*, pp. 148—9 and notes.

Huvelin, *Droit des Marchés et des Foires*, pp. 455—466.

[1] See Appendix, No. v.

As a general rule it was only sales in markets and fairs that during the Middle Ages gave secure possession of stolen goods. The Jews in Germany and Italy were indeed secured in the possession of stolen articles that they had acquired in good faith[1]; it would seem in the Netherlands[2] that bona fide possession was universally protected, and the principle was applied in Hamburg and some other seaport towns[3] to merchandise that came from beyond the seas. But such cases were but exceptions to the common law of the countries of Western Europe. In France and Germany the old Germanic law, that the person from whom goods had been actually stolen had a right of action against third parties, was in the main observed throughout the later centuries of the Middle Ages. "When French and German law take shape in the 13th century, they contain a rule which is sometimes stated by the words 'Mobilia non habent sequelam' ('Les meubles n'ont pas de suite'), or to use a somewhat enigmatical phrase that became current in Germany, 'Hand muss Hand wahren.'......Where I have put my trust, there must I seek it. We have not here to deal with rules which in the interests of Free Trade protect that favourite of modern law, the bona fide purchaser. Neither the positive nor the negative rule pays any heed to good or bad faith. If my goods go from me without my will I can recover

---

[1] Pertile, iv. 258, n. 34. Schroeder, 710 note 9.

[2] Schroeder, 711 and note 12.

[3] Hamburg, Statute of 1270, vii. 9, Breve Pisani communis 1286, Lb. i. rub. 135.

them from the hundredth hand however clean it may be; if they go from me with my will, I have no action against anyone except my bailee[1]." On the other hand in the medieval documents, that mention special rules applicable to sales in market overt, the element of good faith is often expressly recognised[2].

Gradually the privilege was extended in many towns to all the places where commercial transactions were arranged and no longer confined to those concluded in fair or market place[3]. This medieval custom protecting the honest purchaser in open market has passed into the common law of Italy and France, Germany and Austria, and in England a somewhat extended form of the privilege was adopted by the common law. " In the country the market place or piece of ground set apart by custom for the sale of goods is in general the only

---

[1] Pollock and Maitland, *H. E. L.* II. 155.

[2] Huvelin, note 1, p. 462, and note 2, page 463, quotes several examples: among them, Bouteiller, *Somme rural,* "Mais quant à l'usaige coustumier enca la rivière de Somme, s'il est aucun qui ait acheté aucune chose en plein marché *de bonne foi et bien ne congnoisse le vendeur...*"

Coutume de Perpignan. "Item, si quis rem furtivam in nundinis vel in foro vel publice in platea *bona fide* emerit, non cogitur etc...."

Coutume de Vienne. "Non teneatur domino rem suam restituere, etiamsi suam probaverit,...; nisi probaret legitime ipsum emtorem vel creditorem scivisse tempore empcionis rem esse alienam."

Franchise de Genève. "Item si aliquis res mobiles emerit... publice in nundinis, foro et loco publico, infra civitatem, rem furtivam *bona fide et sine fraude.*"

[3] *Franchises de Toulouse,* p. 2. *Rubr. de Empt.* 3. " Quod si aliquis emerit res mobiles in Tolosa publice vel foro, vel in die fori, vel etiam die."; and cf. note 2 above.

market overt there; but in London and in other towns, when so warranted by custom, a sale in an open shop is equivalent to and in fact amounts to a sale in market overt." The rule was developed by the medieval merchant in fair and market, town and seaport, and to him is mainly due the recognition in modern codes of the claims of the bona fide purchaser. He demanded and rightly demanded that in mercantile transactions conducted openly and in the usual resorts of merchants, there should be presumption of good faith. "The practice of merchants," said Lord Bowen, "is not based upon the supposition of possible fraud......Credit, not distrust, is the basis of commercial dealings[1]."

But the idea of good faith, an idea urged by the Church and supported by the merchants, did more than create a rule protecting the honest purchaser in market and fair. Slowly it undermined the Roman and Germanic principle that in general formless contracts are not binding. "The Germanic races not only of the Karlingian period, but down to a much later time, had no general notion whatever of a promise or agreement as a source of civil obligation. Early Germanic law recognised, if we speak in Roman terms, only Formal and Real Contracts. It had not gone so far as to admit a Consensual contract in any case. Sale, for example, was a Real not a Consensual transaction. All recent inquirers seem to concur in accepting this much as having been conclusively

---

[1] Sanders v. McLean, 11, Q.B.D. p. 343. Quoted by Scrutton, *Mercantile Law*, p. 23.

established[1]." In a few cases Roman law enforced the execution of formless agreements, but such cases were exceptional, and the general principle that "nuda pacta" were not obligatory remained an integral part of the system of Roman law. According to the two great systems of law that prevailed in Western Europe a man was not legally bound by a simple promise devoid of legal form. This view the Church strongly opposed, maintaining that a man was bound by his word rather than by the dispositions of the laws, and a great 13th century Canonist writing on pacts declared that according to Canon Law they should be observed in all cases, even though formless, "because between a simple word and an oath .God draws no distinction[2]." The canonical view of the inviolability of agreements gained ground. "All agreements," remarked Beaumanoir who wrote in the 13th century, "are to be kept, for as the saying runs, an agreement overrides law." In the same spirit the Assize of Jerusalem declared that "if any man makes any agreement against the assize and proves it, the agreement made and proved must be kept, for the adage is 'convenant vaine lei[3].'" It was but slowly however that the principle was generally recognised by the civil law. In France it only passed in the 15th century into the treatises on civil law in the work of Panormitain, Archbishop of Palermo, who declared outright "that

---

[1] Pollock and Maitland, *H. E. L.* ii. 185.

[2] Hostiensis, ad tit. de pactis, § quid sit effectus. Quoted by Pollock and Maitland, ii. 195.

[3] Pertile iv. 450, note 1.

a simple promise or agreement is as valid as the stipulations of Roman law[1]." In Germany, while there were attempts here and there from the end of the 13th century onward to override the old formalism of the law of contracts, that formal system on the whole maintained its ground throughout the whole course of the Middle Ages[2]. In England Canon and Roman law early lost the power to shape the development of English law, and "before the end of Edward I.'s reign the King's court had established the rule that the only convention that can be enforced by action is one that is expressed in a written document sealed by the party that is to be charged therewith[3]." "Of informal executory agreements there was in general no remedy in the King's courts[4]."

It would seem however that in commercial disputes the principle of good faith received a wider and earlier application. In Italy it was recognised by Bartolo and Baldo, the great jurists of the 14th century, that, in acts of commerce, informal contracts were binding; and this peculiarity in mercantile usage they attempted to explain by an appeal to the principles of equity; this mercantile usage was repeatedly recognised by later writers[5].

[1] Viollet, *Histoire du droit civil français*, p. 600.

[2] Schroeder, 730. For reception of principle see p. 787.
Heusler, *Privatrecht*, II. 245 and 227.

[3] Pollock and Maitland, II. 219.

[4] Pollock, *Contracts*, 140.

[5] Pertile, IV. 451 note 5.   Goldschmidt, 305, note 33.
Lattes, *Il Diritto Commerciale*, pp. 128 and 129: notes 1—3 give copious references.
St. Calimalae, II. 4. "Pacta et conventiones que *mercatores*

In England it is probable that the local courts took a more liberal view of informal contracts than did the king's justices. " In London a man shall have a writ of covenant without a deed for covenant broken[1]."

The record of the Fair court of St Ives for 1291 presents several cases of disputed contracts in which the parties differed as to the terms of the contract, but in no case is there any reference to a written agreement. The fair courts may indeed have insisted on formalities of some kind or other, but it would seem that written agreements in such matters as partnership or brokerage were not essential. It is quite clear that in the 14th century the validity of nuda pacta in commercial transactions was recognised in Italy by mercantile usage, and it seems probable that in commercial and local courts they were recognised in England.

In Italy it was not as a rule necessary for merchants to state in written contracts the cause of the obligation. The consuls of the Merchant Gild, declare the statutes of Piacenza for the year 1323, are bound and ought to give and render justice (rationem) to any person on any document made or written by the hand of a merchant that shall say: "ego talis debeo tibi tantam pecuniam sicut facerent

Kallismale fecerint inter se unus alteri seu que aliquis mercator fecerit cum tentoribus vel remendatoribus vel *aliis personis* que huic arti non tenerentur *faciemus inviolabiter observari* excepto de ludo taxillorum."

[1] Pollock, *Contracts*, 141, and Pollock and Maitland, II. 222 and note 2.

et redderent de instrumento publici notarii[1]." These
statutes do not stand alone, and several Italian laws
expressly declare that contracts are to be enforced
though the cause is not stated in the written agreement[2]. The statutes refer as a rule to debts "ex
causa negotiationis," but as they expressly state the
contract is to be enforced, even if no cause of debt is
stated, it was inevitable that in practice a "causa"
was not necessary. The merchants wished for perfect freedom of contract. A vast number of medieval
bonds are extant which contain a simple acknowledgement of the debt without cause assigned[3]. It
is perhaps impossible to say that in early medieval
times all the trading countries of Western Europe
had gone as far as the great commercial cities of

[1] Stat. Merc. of Placentia 1323, rubric 10.

[2] Capitula de mercatoribus fugitivis of Milan, 1347. "*Etiam si
causa debiti non sit apposita in illa* scriptura, vel alio modo appareat
debitor seu constet de debito, termino solvendi debitum elapso,
teneatur et debeat solvere creditori. Et hoc statutum locum
habeat in contractibus praeteritis, praesentibus et futuris."

Stat. Merc. of Bergamo 1457. St. di San Marino, II. 10.
"Scripturae privatae contra scribentem habeantur in omnia pro
publico instrumento, etiamsi nulla fuerit expressa causa obliga-
tionis."

St. Merc. Brescia, 1429, c. 107. "Quilibet debitor ex causis
mercantiarum factarum alicui mercatori seu personis, dummodo
constet de debito per cartam...seu scripturam manu debitoris...
etiamsi causa debiti non sit apposita in illa scriptura...debeat
solvere..."

Cf. Goldschmidt, 306, note 36. Lattes, 297, note 9. Pertile,
VI. i. 420, note 64.

[3] Des Marez, *Lettres de Foire*, Documents passim, 13th century. *Monumenta Historiae Patriae*, vol. of Cartae, 12th century
passim. Kurze, *Hanseakten aus England*, Documents, 12 (1288),
45 (1311).

Italy in refusing to recognise the necessity of stating the cause of contracts, but for later times the opinion of Lord Mansfield, that the purely English doctrine of "consideration" did not apply to commercial contracts, is interesting. "A nudum pactum does not exist in the usage and law of merchants. I take it that the ancient notion about the want of consideration was for the sake of evidence only—in commercial cases among merchants the want of consideration is not an objection."

Though acknowledgements of debts in medieval times were often short, containing little besides the amount, the names of creditor and debtor, and the date and place of payment, the written contract for commercial transactions had by the 13th century reached on the continent a high stage of development[1]. "Willingly in order to praise the past has the remark been made," writes M. Blancard in the introduction to his edition of a series of more than one thousand 13th century commercial documents of Marseilles, "that for our forefathers to establish an obligation the spoken word sufficed. If they wished to strengthen the obligation, it was, it has been said, not by a written act but by shaking hands. This assertion cannot apply to the 13th century as the long list of documents which I have edited or analysed proves. Every obligation, even though commercial, was not then based on the spoken word alone, nor on shaking hands, nor even on the kiss of peace when it was in vogue; it was contracted in writing, and not simply and briefly because that would not have presented

[1] Goldschmidt, 151, 152, note 31.

sufficient guarantees, but with a luxury of formulas without connection, or at least out of all proportion with the object of the contract." Though both Church and mercantile usage laid stress upon the binding force of a verbal promise, for the sake of evidence and to prevent misunderstandings contracts were no doubt generally committed to writing. Perhaps the most striking feature in the medieval bonds and contracts is the abundance of clauses safeguarding the interests of the creditor. As a general rule they were in Southern Europe drawn up by public notaries or professional scribes who by the 13th century had become exceedingly numerous and influential. Genoa alone had in the middle of the 13th century 200, Pisa at its close nearly 300, Milan in the following century well over 500, notaries. A single Marseilles notary seems to have drawn up in a single year (1245) more than a thousand commercial documents and on one occasion nearly 60 on a single day[1]. Under the influence of the notaries a uniform legal phraseology—stylus mercatorum—was introduced into the commercial documents of Southern Europe, and this uniformity of language did much to fix and generalise mercantile customs. In many parts of Europe contracts were interpreted by the rules of Roman law, but the universally adopted forms of notarial contracts evaded many of the rules of the law which were not strict enough to satisfy the requirements of the medieval merchant. Almost invariably the debtor

[1] Goldschmidt, 151—2, note 31. Blancard, *Documents Inedits de Marseilles*, Introduction, p. 48.

renounced all the advantages that Roman law conferred upon him: "exceptio non numeratae pecuniae, exceptio rei venditae non traditae, exceptio doli, condictio," privileges of women and many others. Thus in Ypres fair bond (A.D. 1281) the Count of Flanders in the acknowledgement of a debt to merchants of Sienna renounces "in his omnibus et singulis supradictis—privilegio fori et · crucis, exceptioni doli, condictioni indebiti et sine causa vel ex injusta causa, convencioni judicum,—omnique alii juris auxilio canonici et civilis, cunctisque aliis exceptionibus, constitutionibus, dilationibus, defensionibus, et cujuscunque alterius juris auxiliis": and in another, two Ypres merchants renounce in favour of their debtor Bertram de Fort, citizen of Rochelle, "a tous privileges de Sainte Englise et de croise prise et a prendre et a tous plais de cristiente et de loi mondaine et a toutes les coses qui dendroit ce paiement leur poroient eidier et valoir, et le devant dit Bertram le Fort greveir ou nuire[1]." In the Marseilles contracts the renunciations are most numerous and detailed. To England "the Lombard merchants have brought with them precedents for bonds, lengthy, precise and stringent forms which they compel their English debtors to execute[2]." In England however the continental system of public notaries never gained a firm footing. The system had great advantages; the notary[3] was a public

---

[1] Des Marez, *Lettres de Foire à Ypres*, Documents 84 and 46, cf. Nos. 23, 34, 74, 93, 127, 140, 149, 157.

[2] Pollock and Maitland, I. 219.

[3] Pertile VI. part i. p. 416, note 40, and p. 295. Bresslau, *Urkundenlehre*, traces the institution from late Roman Empire, ch. 8.

official, originally appointed only by Pope or
Emperor; when princes, bishops and cities were
granted or had usurped the right of appointment,
the notary still retained his rank of a public officer.
Documents drawn up by a public notary were regarded by the law as authentic[1].

Other means however were available for securing
the recognition of contracts and bonds by the public
authorities. The "fair bond" seems to have been
extremely common in North-Western Europe, and
over 7000 of these bonds dating from 1249–1291
have been discovered at Ypres alone. It is probable
that until 1275 or thereabouts the Ypres bonds were
not drawn up by official scribes, but from 1283
onwards the bonds are the handiwork of a small
body of clerks who must have been the clerks of the
town. But both before and after this change the
bonds were as a rule authentic documents because
they were almost invariably drawn up in the presence of the town echevins. The number of the
magistrates present varied; it was generally two but
occasionally five or six. The fair bond then became
a kind of public document. "A proof of the obligation became superfluous; the recognition of the debt
before the magistrates gave it full and entire credence,

---

[1] Bresslau, *Urkundenlehre*, 493: "das Ende der Entwickelung
ist, dass die von einem öffentlichen Notar ausgefertigte formell
echte Urkunde ein Instrumentum publicum, dass heisst, ein mit
publica fides ausgestattetes Aktenstuck wird, das die in ihm aus
amtlicher Wahrnehmung bezeugten Thatsachen *unbedingt beweist*."

Pertile, vi. i. p. 417—18 and notes 48—51. Stat. Antiq.
Romae, iii. 112, "Nulla persona audeat opponere aliquam excep-
tionem contra instrumentum scriptum manu notarii Romani."

and no proof could prevail against it[1]." At the
great fairs of Champagne the same expedient was
adopted and the bonds were passed before the
guards of the fair, who impressed them with the fair
seal. Originally it was not necessary for fair debts
to be so authenticated. The customs of the fair
at first allowed anyone to bind himself "en la
foire soulz le scel et sans le scel de la foire," and
debts contracted during the fair could be proved
by witness. "Item au prouver sa debte, faudra
instrument scelle du scel desdites foires ou enregistre
ou registre d'icelles, ou deulx tesmoings qui temoig-
neront par une voye ou par gaige de bataille[2]."
But a desire to avoid frauds, and to increase the
revenues of the fairs, led to a change in the law
and customs of the Champagne fairs. All bonds for
debts contracted during the fairs were to be authenticated by the fair seal. The ordinance of 1349 was
most precise and established that "toutes les lecttres
touchant le faict et action des foires qui ne seront
scellee du scel desdites foires, exceptez les memoriaux
et actes des parties tant seulement, soit de nul effect,
ny a icelles lettres aucune foi soit adjoustee." Once
sealed the bond was valid and could only be repu-
diated by proving that the fair seal had been forged.
"Scel authentique fait foi par la coutume." But for
the bonds of the Champagne fairs the seal not only
served as a proof of the authenticity of the docu-

[1] Des Marez, *op. cit.*, p. 40 and 17 and 13.
[2] The quotations from "Les coustumes, stille et usaige" of the
Champagne Fairs are taken from Huvelin, *Droit des Marchés*,

ments, it also gave them executive force throughout the French kingdom. Nor was this all. The international importance of the Champagne fairs gave to their bonds a special value, and at Piacenza statutes of 1336 declare that "litterae nundinarum Campanie et Brie" should have the evidential value and the same executive force as public documents[1]. In England the legislation of Edward I. provided a ready and · efficient method of authenticating the debts of merchants and securing their payment. Though the two statutes of 1283 and 1285 were not confined to merchants or to debts arising out of mercantile transactions, the preamble to both statutes shows that they were enacted in the interests of the merchant classes ; and in 1311 upon complaint that the statutes, though favourable to the great merchants, were found to press hard upon the people, the regulations of the statutes were limited to contracts between merchants[2]. The two acts are of great importance in the history of the Law Merchant in England. Though enacted in Parliament and intended before their modification in 1311 to apply to debts of every kind throughout the realm, they yet mark a development in the law that was observed in the special commercial courts and enforced in the case of commercial debt. The use of English statute law, and the frequent employment that has been made of the statutes and customs of individual cities as evidence for the rules of Law Merchant which has

---

[1] Huvelin, p. 480.

[2] Kurze, *Hanseakten aus England* (Hansische Geschichtsquellen, Band vi.), Introduction, pp. 28, 29.

been declared to be distinct from the common law, may perhaps require explanation.

The Law Merchant was no doubt a special body of law. It was the law observed by merchants, to a large extent created by them, and distinct in England from the common law of the land and from the usages and customs of individual cities. Of this there can be no doubt and it is recognised in the most unmistakable terms by the Statute of the Staple of Edward III.'s reign which ordains (cap. 8) " that all merchants coming to the Staple, their servants and their meiny in the Staple shall be ruled by the law merchant in all things touching the Staple and not by the common law of the land, nor by the usage of boroughs, cities and other towns." But though the Law Merchant was thus a separate system of law, distinct from the common law, distinct from individual town customs, it was by means of the central authority that the law was sometimes altered or authoritatively declared; and while it cannot be asserted that a commercial usage of any individual town, however great or however important that town might be, formed a rule of the Law Merchant, the usages of the great commercial cities tended to conform to the general usage of merchants throughout Europe. The Law Merchant of medieval times was the system of rules actually enforced in the commercial courts and actually observed by merchants in their dealings with one another, just as Modern International Law is the system of rules actually observed by modern States in the relations of State to State. The treaties, the

legislation, and the actions of individual States do
not necessarily conform to the generally recognised
rules of International Law, but they may be and
are used as evidence to establish what those rules
really are.   In the same way the Statute Law of
medieval states, the ordinances of medieval kings,
and the usages of medieval law, need not conform,
in any particular case, to the commercial regulations
generally enforced among medieval merchants, but
they may be used to establish the general usages
of merchants in commercial cases.   Both International Law and the Law Merchant are from their
very nature vague and uncertain.   In modern times
great nations have held views diametrically opposed
upon the rules of International Law in not unim-
portant matters.   In medieval times the merchants
were not rarely at a loss when called upon to declare
the law, and occasionally craved time for consideration.
For the rules of International Law and of the Law
Merchant depend mainly upon the general practice;
and if with numberless treatises on International
Law the international rule even in modern times
can often only be regarded as a moot question, there
can be no wonder if the medieval merchant was at
times uncertain as to the rule of the Law Merchant.
To a modern enquirer the task of determining what
is a general principle of the Law Merchant and
what is merely a local or national usage is far more
difficult than it was to the medieval merchant in
a medieval court.   The attempt however has to be
made, and everything that throws light upon the
commercial customs and usages of the time has to

be taken into consideration. The commercial statutes of any individual country or city are not the Law Merchant, but that law at times found expression in those statutes. The usages of any particular town never conformed entirely to the usages generally observed in every country; but collectively the customs of the great commercial cities of Europe form valuable material from which may be deduced by careful comparison what were probably the general usages. Moreover while the Law Merchant was in its broadest sense the body of commercial rules observed throughout Western Christendom, it must be remembered that each country developed to a certain extent upon its own lines. There is a sense in which an "English Law Merchant" may be said to have existed. The Law Merchant as observed in England was always slowly changing; often that change was due to the influence of changes that had taken place in the commercial usages of other countries and was effected by decisions in the special commercial courts in fairs or staple town or seaport where foreign merchants abounded and had a right to express their views of the law, forming half of or all the "mercati" of the court when a foreigner is a party, or the case is between foreigners: sometimes on the other hand the change was effected by royal authority, and it was by royal authority that the English system of recognition and enforcement of debt was brought into closer harmony with the usages and laws that already prevailed on the continent. "Bonds of record," a speedy process of execution, and the liability of the debtor's property both real and personal, were recognised maxims in the continental countries of Western Europe, and these were the maxims enforced by Edward's legislation of 1283 and 1285. "Forasmuch," declares the statute of Acton Burnell of the year 1283, "Merchants which heretofore have lent their goods to divers persons be greatly impoverished because there is no speedy Law provided for them to have recovery of their debts at the day of payment assigned, and by reason hereof many merchants have withdrawn to come into this realm with their merchandises, to the damage as well of the merchants as of the whole realm, the king by himself and by his council hath ordained and established, That the Merchant which will be sure of his debt shall cause his debtor to come before the Mayor of London, or of York, or Bristol, or before the Mayor and a clerk which the king shall appoint for the same, for to knowledge the debt and the day of payment, and the recognisance shall be entered into a roll with the hand of the said clerk, which shall be known. Moreover the said clerk shall make with his own hand a Bill Obligatory whereunto the seal of the debtor shall be put with the king's seal, that shall be provided for the same purpose, the which seal shall remain in the keeping of the Mayor and clerk aforesaid. And if the debtor doth not pay at the day to him limited, the creditor may come before the said Mayor and clerk with his Bill Obligatory, and if it be found by the roll and by the bill that the debt was knowledged and that the day of payment is expired, the Mayor shall incontinent cause the

moveables of the debtor to be sold, as far as the
debt doth amount by the praising of honest men,
as Chattels and Burgages devisable until the whole
sum of the debt, and the money without delay shall
be paid to the creditor. And if the Mayor can find
no buyer, he shall cause the moveables to be
delivered to the creditor at a reasonable price, as
much as doth amount to the sum of the debt in
allowance of his debt. And the king's seal shall be
put unto the sale and deliverance of the Burgages
devisable for a perpetual witness. And if the debtor
have no moveables within the jurisdiction of the
Mayor whereupon the debt may be levied, but have
some otherwhere within the realm, then shall the
Mayor send the recognisance made before him and
the clerk aforesaid unto the chancellor under the
king's seal. And the chancellor shall direct a writ
unto the sheriff in whose bailiwick the moveables of
the debtor be, and the sheriff shall cause him to
agree with his creditor in such form as the Mayor
should have done in case the moveables of the
debtor had been within his power. And let
them that praise the moveable goods to be delivered
unto the creditor take good heed that they do set
a reasonable price upon them; for if they do set an
overhigh price for favour born to the debtor and to
the damage of the creditor, then shall the thing so
praised be delivered unto themselves at such price
as they have limited, and they shall forthwith be
answerable unto the creditor for his debt. And if
the debtor have no moveables whereupon his debt
may be levied, then shall his body be taken where

it may be found and kept in prison until he have made agreement, or his friends for him." Two years later the regulations of the law of 1283 were reenacted and in addition the immoveable property of the debtor was made liable. "And within a quarter of a year after that he is taken," ordains the statute of 1285, "his chattels and lands shall be delivered to him so that by his own he may levy and pay his debt. And it shall be lawful unto him during the same quarter to sell his lands and tenements for the discharge of his debts, and his sale shall be good and effectual. And if he do not agree within the quarter, next after the quarter expired, all the lands and goods of the debtor shall be delivered unto the merchant by a reasonable extent to hold them until such time as the debt is levied....And the merchant shall have such seisin in the lands and tenements delivered unto him or his assignee that he may maintain a writ of Novel Disseisin if he is put out....And if in case the sheriff return that the debtor cannot be found or that he is clerk, the merchant shall have writs to all the sheriffs where he shall have land....And a seal shall be provided that shall serve for fairs and the same shall be sent unto every fair." Similarly the Ordinance of the Staple (1353) gave power to the Mayor of the staple "to take recognisances of debts which a man will make him," "to the intent that contracts made within the same staple shall be the better holden and the payments readily made[1]." The procedure was however made somewhat more severe; execution

---

[1] Keble, cap. 9.

was to proceed "in manner as it is contained in the
Statute Merchant" (1285), but the debtor was to
"have no advantage of the quarter of a year which
is contained in the said Statute Merchant."

Originally immoveables had not in Germanic law
been liable for debt. This principle of Germanic law
was already losing ground in the times of the
Carlovingians[1], and in Italy[2], France and Germany[3]
the lands of a debtor were by the 13th century liable
as a general rule for the debts of their owner, though
in many cases they could only be seized after the

[1] Brunner, *Deutsche Rechtsgeschichte*, ii. 459, 460; in note 20
(p. 460) Brunner refers to a charter cited in note 41 on p. 74 as
the plainest evidence "dass die Entstehung der Immobiliarexe-
cution in der Konfiskation friedlosen Gutes ihren rechtgeschicht-
lichen Ausgangspunkt hatte."

Cf. Pertile, vi. ii. p. 330.

[2] v. Pertile, vi. ii. 331. On p. 338 and 339, notes 55 and 56,
Pertile quotes *inter alia* the following: Const. leg. Pisanae Civitatis (A.D. 1231). "Data la sentenza, si apud reum, vel alium
pro eo, res ipsa mobilis vel immobilis invenitur, per consulem
justitie victori, et in ipsius potestatem statim tribuatur."

Stat. of Vercelli, A.D. 1241. "Si quis ad postulationem
creditoris consignaverit bona sua et de rebus mobilibus non
consignavit tantum unde possit satisfieri creditoribus, tunc de
rebus immobilibus...satisfaciat creditoribus ejus...."

[3] Stadtrecht Münster-Bielefeld (circa 1221), cap. 44. Keutgen,
Urkunden, p. 153. "Si quis obtinuerit sentenciis, quod debet
ostendere res de quibus debitor suus ei possit solvere, non licet ei
ostendere super vestes suas et sue uxoris et ejus suppelectilem,
si habet wicbelethe (*i.e.* lands held by burgage tenure) vel alias
res."

In Hamburg the landed property of citizens was by Stadtrecht
of 1262 (c. 22) made liable for debt. See *Das Handlungsbuch*,
'Vickos von Geldersen,' edited by Norrnheim, Introduction,
p. xxx.

Schroeder, *Rechtsgeschichte*, p. 767.

moveables had been taken and found insufficient.
The process of change was slow and during the
period of transformation the usage varied in different
parts of the same kingdom. In several provinces,
writes Viollet in his History of French Law, "in the
12th and sometimes even in the 13th century the
movable property of the debtor alone was liable for
his obligations." In Belgium[1] "immoveables were
often pledged as a security in commercial transactions." The whole tendency of mercantile usage
was to secure the creditor in every way possible.
This tendency is not only seen in the introduction of
a prompt process of execution and the liability of
landed property for the payment of debt: it also
appears in the solidarity stipulated in mercantile
contracts for sureties and in cases where there were
several principal debtors. Among the thousands of
fair bonds discovered at Ypres there are but few in
which debtors are bound only for their own part, and
when this is the case the responsibility of each
debtor is defined most scrupulously. As a general
rule where there is more than one debtor in these
bonds[2] the debtors bind themselves "chascun por le
tout," and when there were several sureties in the
same way each was surety for the whole debt[3].

---

[1] Des Marez, *La Lettre de Foire*, pp. 40—52. Des Marez,
La Propriété Foncière dans les Villes du Moyen Age, pp. 252, 253.

[2] Des Marez, *La Lettre de Foire*, pp. 40—42 and documents,
nos. 9, 10, 11, 13, 17, 23, 40, 43, 46, 64, 74, 82, 94, 118, 121, 131,
153, 154.

[3] Des Marez, nos. 8, 18, 43, 44 B, 53, 55, 61, 64, 70, 83, 88,
89, 92, 94, 99, 105, 109, 118, 120, 139.

There is the same solidarity[1] of creditor in the commercial documents of Italy, of Marseilles and numerous other towns, and the formularies in the "summa artis notariae" of Rolandinus, a work which exercised a vast influence upon the form of legal documents throughout the Middle Ages, contains the customary formula, "unusquisque ipsorum principaliter et in solidum sine aliqua exceptione juris." But mercantile practice went further than this in the early Middle Ages. A merchant was held responsible in other cities and in other lands for the debts of his fellow townsman. The usage however ran counter to the real interests of the trading classes, and a series of laws, ordinances, royal charters, and treaties gradually abolished this burdensome custom. Early in his reign Edward I. declared that the rule should not apply to English merchants in English cities and fairs, and the Ordinance of the Staple issued in the middle of the reign of Edward III. extended the privilege, though with a saving clause that may have robbed it of much of its value, to foreign merchants. The 17th chapter of this ordinance declares "that no merchant stranger be impeached for another's trespass or for another's debt whereof he is not debtor, pledge nor mainpernour, provided always that if our liege people, merchants or other, be indamaged by any lords of strange lands or their subjects, and the said lords duly required fail of right to our said subjects, we shall have the law of Marque and the taking of them

[1] See references in Goldschmidt, p. 309, note 41, and p. 284 and notes. Among these are the English bonds published by Bond in *Archaeologia*, vol. xxviii. (London, 1840).

again, as hath been used in times passed without
fraud or deceit." The same tendency was evident
in other countries. "In 1193 Philip Augustus takes
under his protection the merchants of Ypres and their
merchandise throughout the extent of his realm. In
future they cannot be arrested either for the debts
of their fellow citizens or for those of the Court of
Flanders, unless they had become sureties[1]." Queen
Elizabeth of Hungary[2], in consequence of the complaints of the merchants of Vienna and Austria,
promised in a royal charter of the year 1381 that
when Austrian merchants came into Hungary for
purposes of trade they should not be arrested and
condemned for the debts and misdeeds of others.
In Italy a long series of treaties between the great
commercial cities attempted during the 13th century
to limit this right of reprisal, and of this policy
Florence made itself the leader during the 14th
century[3]. The statutes of the important Calimala
gild (1301) instructed the consuls to call as quickly
as they·could a special council, or if they preferred,
a general council, "and to take counsel with them
as to what was to be done with the cases of
reprisals in divers lands in which our merchants

---

[1] Des Marez, *La Lettre de Foire*, p. 43.

[2] *Quellen zur Geschichte der Stadt Wien*, II. i. number 1002.

[3] See Bonolis, *La Giurisdizione della Mercanzia in Firenze nel secolo xiv.*, especially pp. 96 and 97.

Del Vecchio, *Le Rappresaglie nei Comuni Medievali special-mente in Firenze*, especially pp. 230—252 and the documents in appendices.

Arias, *I Trattati Commerciali della Repubblica Fiorentina*, pp. 156—229, and documents in Appendix.

often suffer loss." " They shall take good heed," the
statute continues, "that the reprisals are settled, and
that all the citizens of Florence by reason of whom
reprisals have been granted against other citizens shall
effectually be compelled to give satisfaction so that
the men of Florence do not suffer further loss." " The
consuls moreover are in duty bound to assemble and
meet with the captains of the seven greater gilds
and petition...that it may be established by the council of the commune of Florence that no reprisal be
granted or conceded to any person on behalf of the
commune of Florence save in the presence of the
seven captains[1]." A few years later the councillors
of the Mercanzia were ordered to arrange with the
authorities of the city that " treaties be made with
any land and community of Tuscany or elsewhere as
might seem good to the five councillors that as
between the commune of Florence and the said
communes reprisals cannot and shall not be granted
or conceded for any cause save in case of robbery
only[2]." During the course of the 15th century
reprisals against merchants were rapidly growing
rarer, and in 1474 the Emperor ordered the restora-
tion of goods taken by way of reprisal from a Jew,
while Henry V. of England de ' ed any unjust
aggression against foreigners high treason[3]. The
system of reprisals forms part both of the Law Merchant and of " Private International Law." It forms

---

[1] St. Calimalae (1301), Lb. iv. c. 30.

[2] Statuto della Mercanzia del 1312. Rubrics 6, 14, 23 printed
in *Del Vecchio*.

[3] Pertile, i. p. 265, note 67, and *Del Vecchio*, pp. 87, 88.

part of the Law Merchant in that the system was recognised and enforced in the special commercial courts of the Middle Ages, and because it corresponded to the peculiar character of commercial enterprise during early medieval times when towns and their gilds formed close economic units, united for purposes of trade, supporting their members against other cities in their just demands and consequently held liable, and at first justly held liable, for the misdeeds and debts of their own citizens and members. The communal spirit which was so strong was evident in other ways, and townsman or gildsman had a right to a share in any bargain made in his presence[1]. This spirit was however growing antiquated, and the growth of the principle that the merchant was not liable for the debts of his fellow citizens but only for those for which he had become surety, marks a distinct advance alike in the Law Merchant and in International Law.

.During the Middle Ages contracts of partnership were common, and at their close companies with freely alienable shares 'had come into existence. In the early centuries the most common form of partnership was the "commenda." This was a partnership in which one of the parties supplied the capital either in the shape of money or goods, without personally taking an active part in the operations of the society, while the other party supplied none or only a smaller fraction of the capital and conducted the actual trade

---

[1] Bateson, *Records of Leicester*, p. xxxii. and p. 271.

Faigniez, *Documents relatifs à l'histoire de l'industrie et du commerce en France*, vol. i. No. 210 (Paris), vol. ii. No. 71.

of the association. This form of partnership was
especially used in maritime trade and was often confined to single ventures. Its popularity was due to
the fact that it enabled the capitalist to turn his
money to good account without violating the canonical laws against usury, and the small merchant
or shipper to secure credit and to transfer the risk of
the venture to the capitalist. The nature of the
contract will best be shown by quoting one or two
examples of the vast number of these contracts that
have been preserved.

The following is a Marseilles contract of the year
1210 :

"Notum sit cunctis quod ego Bonetus Pellicerius
confiteor et recognosco me habuisse et recepisse in
comanda, a te Stephano de Mandoil et a te Bernardo
Baldo, xxv l. regalium coronatorum...quas ego
portabo ad laborandum in hoc itinere Bogie, in nave
de Estella, vel ubicumque navis ierit causa negoti-
andi, ad vestrum proficuum et meum, ad fortunam
dei et ad usum maris, et totum lucrum et capitale
convenio et promitto reducere in potestatem
vestri et vestrorum fideliter, et veritatem inde vobis
dicam, et ita hoc me observaturum in mea bona fide
per stipulationem promitto, et in omni lucro quod
Deus ibi dederit, debeo habere et accipere quartum
denarium[1]."

Such contracts were not rare in Italy in the 12th

[1] *Documents Inédits sur le Commerce de Marseilles au Moyen
Age*, by Blancard, Document 4, vol. i. p. 7. There are scores of
similar contracts of Commenda in these two volumes, and there
are numerous 12th century examples in the volume of Chartae in
the *Monumenta Historiae Patriae*.

century and the contracts are to the same intent as those of Marseilles in the 13th century. "March 1155. Ego Petrus de Tolosi profiteor me accepisse a te Ottone Bono libras centum viginti septem quas debeo portare laboratum Salernum vel ex hinc apud Siceliam, et de proficuo quod ibi deus dederit debeo habere quartam et reditum debeo mittere in tua potestate[1]."

Often when both parties to the contract contributed to the capital of the association the partnership was termed "collegantia," or "societas" to distinguish it from the more common form of commenda in which the commendator alone supplied the funds.

"Bonus Johannes Malfuastus et Bonus Senior Rubeus contraxerunt societatem, in quam Bonus Johannes libras 34 et Bonus Senior libras 16 contulit. Hanc societatem portare debet Alexandriam laboratum nominatus Bonus Senior et inde Januam venire debet. Capitali extracto proficuum et persone (?) per medium. Ultra confessus est nominatus Bonus Senior quod portat de rebus nominati Boni Johannis libr. 20 sol. 13 de quibus debet habere quartam proficui—. Juravit insuper ipse Bonus Senior quod supradictam societatem et commendacionem diligenter salvabit et promovebit societatem ad proficuum sui et Boni johannis et commendacionem ad proficuum ipsius Boni johannis et quod societatem omnem et ipsam commendacionem et proficuum in potestatem reducet ipsius Boni Johannis[2]."

[1] *Monumenta Historiae Patriae*, Chartae, column 287.
[2] Goldschmidt, p. 260 and note 88 b.

But whether the commendator alone or both parties contributed to the capital, the association remained essentially of the same character. The commendator in both cases was a kind of sleeping partner, and it was left to the "tractator" to carry out all the necessary operations. Though the partnership was generally formed for the purpose of a definite speculation, it was also formed for an indefinite series of commercial transactions, or for an indefinite or sometimes a definite time, which was occasionally as long as 10 years[1].

As a rule the commendator who supplied the capital took the risk of the transaction; if the goods were lost he could not recover the amount 'he had advanced, provided that the contract contained the usual clause "ad risicum et fortunam Dei, maris et gentium," or its equivalent.. The usual share in the profits of a tractator who brought no capital into the partnership was a quarter, while in the case where he contributed to the general fund, his share of the profits amounted to a half. It is hard to tell whether the "tractator" in early times always traded in his own name, though there is no doubt that in later times he did[2]. Pertile holds the view that originally the tractator was regarded as a mere factor of the commendator who was responsible for the acts of the tractator, but that gradually in the course of time the principle was established that he was only responsible to the amount of the capital

---

[1] Goldschmidt, p. 264.
[2] Goldschmidt, p. 265 and note 104. Lattes, p. 157.

which he had advanced[1]. In Florence this principle
was definitely established by statute in 1408. In
the medieval commenda was represented both the
dormant partner and the principle of limited
liability of modern times. The commenda was not
confined to England: it existed during the Middle
Ages in Germany and Scandinavia[2]. In cases where
there were several commendators who entrusted
their capital to one or more tractators, the latter
began to assume a more independent position towards
commendators. Contracting in their own name the
managers were responsible for the debts of the
association, while the commendators were freed, in
Florence as early as 1408, from all liability beyond
the amount of their quota. This type of commenda
was a natural development of the simple original
type in which there were but two persons involved,
—a single commendator who advanced the capital to a
single tractator; but it was an important development,
and in the 16th century it was regulated in Italy by
several city statutes and in the following century in
France by regulation[3]. Thus regulated the society
contained both members with limited liability and
members with unlimited liability, and it was the
latter that controlled the administration of the
society. The older and simpler form of commenda,

[1] Pertile, IV. 685, 686, note 24. Cf. Viollet, *Histoire du droit
civil français*, p. 762. "Dans la société le bailleur de fonds ou
commendataire n'est passible des pertes que jusqu'à concurrence
des fonds qu'il a mis ou dû mettre dans la société."

[2] Norrnheim, *Geldersen's Handlungsbuch*, Introduction, 43—5.
Amira, *Nordgermanisches Obligationesrecht*, vol. II.

[3] Goldschmidt, 269. Lattes, p. 162 and notes.

however, existed side by side with the newer and more complex type. Of the newer type the modern "Société en commandite" is the historical descendant and it is characterised by the same essential features, the existence of two classes of members, the one with a responsibility limited to the amount of the capital they have contributed, and the other with an unlimited liability for the debts of the society, the administration of which lies solely in their hands[1]. On the other hand the commendator of the older and simple type of commenda has his counterpart in the dormant partner of modern commercial law.

But side by side with the commenda there existed throughout the Middle Ages a closer kind of partnership in which the partners were normally coordinate members of the association with the same privileges and responsibilities. The usual expression for this type of society was "compagnia" or "societas," and the firm was generally designated by the name of one of its members with the addition of the phrase "et socii," or the like. It became an essential feature of this form of partnership that the partners were all of them responsible individually for the debts of the firm[2]. At no time in Italy was the power of partners to bind by contract their fellow partners in practice denied[3]. The principle of direct representation was thus admitted, and Baldo writing in the 14th century declared "ex consuetudine mercatorum unus socius scribit nomen alterius[4]." Baldo however adds that

---

[1] V. Thaller, *Traité Élémentaire de Droit Commercial*, §§ 258—262, pp. 160—162.

[2] Lattes, p. 161 and notes. [3] Cf. however pp. 132—135 below.

[4] Goldschmidt, p. 276, note 139.

M.

this was "abusio." This was an important advance upon the principles of both Roman and old Germanic law, neither of which recognised sufficiently the principle of direct representation. "All this view of the law," says Kohler writing of the principle of representation, "appears altogether artificial and cannot well appeal to primitive man : he cannot understand a transaction (based) upon the will of another ; even a developed law like Roman law has only developed 'representation' very imperfectly and German law long resisted it[1]." Medieval merchants and mercantile usage recognised the principle of representation ; they recognised it not only in the right of one partner to make contracts binding upon the other partners of a firm, they also recognised it in the medieval bills of exchange with their clauses to order or bearer.

As the names of all the partners did not appear[2] in the name of the firm, but were simply referred to generally in the phrase "et socii" or some equivalent expression, it became important to determine

[1] Kohler, 'Zivilrecht' in *Holtzendorff's Encyklopädie der Rechtswissenschaft*, vol. I. p. 598. Kohler quotes from and refers to many Italian authorities of 12—14th century on representation. Among them St. Como (A.D. 1232). "Tantum valeat et prosit illi, ad cujus partem vel cujus nomine facta est vel recepta, ac si illam cartam vel contractum vel obligationem recepisset."

St. of Brescia, regulation of A.D. 1252 in St. of 1313. "Quod ex omni contractu inito et facto nomine alterius, tam de mercato quam de aliis rebus, acquiratur actio et acquisita sit illi vel illis, quorum vel cujus nomine contractus sive promissio factus est vel facta."

[2] Bartolus. "Secundum consuetudinem et fere totius Italiae— litteris mercatorum unus nominatur nomine proprio et omnes alii nomine appellativo, hoc modo: Titius et socius talis societatis," quoted by Goldschmidt, p. 276, note 137.

who were to be legally regarded as members of
the firm. In early Italian statutes actual common
trading of the persons concerned, or general notoriety,
sufficed to prove the partnership: "et intellegantur
socii qui in eadem statione vel negotiatione morantur
vel mercantur ad invicem[1]." In doubtful cases the
books of the firm were consulted[2]. But general
notoriety and the books of the firm were not found
sufficient either to protect the general public against
partners who denied the partnership altogether or
who asserted that the partnership had been dissolved,
or to protect merchants from a general liability for all
the debts of a trader with whom they occasionally
combined for the purpose of a common speculation.
Dissolution of partnerships was to be valid only if
effected "per instrumentum publicum." If any one
practising in the Calimala craft," says a Florentine
gild statute of 1301, "or having a share in any
'societas' of that craft has renounced or shall
renounce it in the future, such renunciation shall
not be valid nor be admitted by the consuls, unless
he shall show that he withdrew from that firm by
means of a public document, and the consuls shall
have that document published throughout the whole
craft." Registration of partners became usual; from
the 14th century onwards such registers were kept
not merely by the gilds but by the city authorities;

---

[1] St. Mutinae, 1327, quoted among others by Goldschmidt,
276, notes 140 and 141.

[2] St. of Calimala of Florence, Lb. ii. rubric 43. "Si quis...
librum corporis sue societatis celavit vel celaverit ita quod haberi
et videri non possit quod sit sotii (sic) dicte societatis." Cf. Lattes,
p. 174, note 59 and p. 283.

and the registration required, as a rule, "the direct intervention either personally or by special procuration of all the members of the firm[1]."

It has been stated that one partner could represent the rest and make contracts binding upon the whole firm, and that this was an advance upon the principles of Roman and Germanic law, which only recognised representation to a limited degree. But though a single partner could thus represent the firm, originally it was as a rule only in virtue of special procuration that he was privileged so to do. In the medieval contracts of partnership the partners often gave one another by procuration the right to represent and bind the firm. In the absence of such clauses in the contract creditors of the firm for a debt contracted by an individual partner could in some places only make good their claim against the firm as a whole, if the debt had been recognised as a debt of the firm, as by entry in the firm's book, or employment of the money or goods for the common purposes of the firm. Simply in his capacity as partner a merchant had not everywhere in the early centuries of the Middle Ages a right to bind his copartners. "Whoever in the city or district of Florence," declares a Florence gild regulation of the year 1236, " has sold cloth or other things pertaining to trade to any one of this gild cannot seek nor sue for the money or price of the sale from any of the partners of the buyer, or from any one of his firm, unless the money shall be found written in the books of the buyer's firm as payable for the price of that

[1] Lattes, p. 162 and note 68.

sale[1]." Similarly the gild statute of Verona for the
year 1318 required the tacit consent of the other
partners or an express promise on their part to pay
—"nec praejudicet etiam stando in statione et essendo
socius palam; dummodo non esset praesens cum
socio ad accipiendam mercandiam et non promitteret
de solvendo eam."

As late as the 15th century the jurist Alexander
Tartagnus denies the responsibility of the other
partners, unless the contract had been made with
full powers "nomine societatis[2]." Slowly however
the principle gained ground that a partner had as
partner the right to make contracts binding upon
his firm. In all probability this change was due to
the frequency with which the individual partner was
entrusted with this power by special procuration.
Thus in one of the Marseilles documents of the 13th
century which have been already referred to, two
partners concede full powers to the third. "Nos
Dietavivo Alberto et Guidaloto Guidi, Senenses
facimus, constituimus, ordinamus, Bellinchonum
Charrenconi, consocium nostrum, absentem, nostrum
certum et generalem procuratorem in omnibus

---

[1] St. of Calimala, 1301, Lb. ii. rubric 19. The date 1236 is
given in the rubric.

[2] Goldschmidt, 281, note 154. Goldschmidt gives many
quotations from and references to city and gild statutes, *inter
alia* St. of Calimala Gild (1341). "E niuno mercantante di
questa arte possa obligare in Firenze o nel distretto la sua
compagnia o alcuno compagno della sua compagnia—se non in
debiti o cose che fossono scritte nel libro o libri della sua
compagnia, o se almeno due o più de' compagni non fossono
insieme a tale obligazione fare, o se non avese in ciò speciale
o generale procurazione e mandato da' suoi compagni."

nostris negotiis peragendis,......promittentes nos
ratum perpetuo habitaturos quicquid cum eo vel per
eum actum fuerit in praemissis, sub obligacione
omnium bonorum meorum praesentium et futuro-
rum[1]." Such procurations were exceedingly common[2], and the great Calimala Gild of Florence went
so far as to iustruct (1301) all its members when
they sent any one abroad to transact business to provide them with a special or general procuration. The
result was that in actual practice the partner did have
power to bind the firm, and that gradually this power
was regarded as a matter of course. During the 14th
and 15th centuries numerous Italian statutes recognised the responsibility of the other partners for the
debts and contracts made by an individual member
of the firm. But both the doctrine of the great civil
jurists and the decisions of isolated commercial courts
were long opposed to this new view of the position
of the partner. Thus the decisions of the "Rota of
Genoa" only go so far as to say that whatever is
written by one of them having the "facultas" of using
the name of the firm is said to be written by the firm
itself, while another decision declares most plainly
that such "facultas" is not to be taken as a matter
of course. By the 17th century however the power
of an individual partner, though without special
procuration, to act in the name of his firm was
admitted by the civil jurists[3]. The unlimited

[1] Blancard, op. cit., no. 115.

[2] See numerous quotations and references in Goldschmidt,
p. 282, note 155.

[3] De Luca, De Camb., disc. 29, nos. 3, 4, quoted Goldschmidt,
p. 283.

liability of the partner for the debts of the firm was, like the right of the partner as partner to represent the firm, of gradual growth, and was not in the early centuries of the Middle Ages universally enforced by the law[1]. In medieval contracts unlimited liability was indeed often stipulated and was in some places a maxim of the law : in the fairs of Champagne, for example, the unlimited responsibility of partners was under certain conditions expressly recognised ; the "usage of the fairs" declared that a partner "oblige tous leurs biens (*i.e.* the partners) pour cause de l'administration qu'il a et qu'il semble avoir, et plus, se aulcun des compaignons se boute en franchise ou destourne ses biens ou les biens de sa compagnye, il est oblige et tout li autre compaignon qui paravant cette fuite ou tel destournement des biens n'estoient obligez en corps et en biens par la coustume, stille et usaige des foires notoires[2]." It was not however till towards the close of the 16th century that the solidarity of partners was in Italy generally recognised. "Only gradually and without the support of positive law the liability of every partner 'in solidum' came through mercantile usage to be enforced in statutes and judicial decisions. This liability was repeatedly recognised in the decisions of Genoa. Since that time it was never a matter of doubt[3]," and in the 17th century the jurist Ansaldus who, as auditor of the Roman Rota, must have had a

---

[1] Goldschmidt, pp. 284 and 288 and note 159.

[2] Goldschmidt, 285, note 160.

[3] Endemann, *Studien in der romanisch-kanonistischen Wirtschafts- und Rechtslehre*, vol. I. p. 395.

thorough acquaintance with judicial decisions in commercial cases, recognised this unlimited liability and declared that in the first place the creditor had recourse to the capital of the firm, and only in the second place could he avail himself of the unlimited liability of the individual partner[1]. The commenda and the societas had an independent origin and an independent development. Originally the commenda was a purely speculative enterprise, confined mainly at first to maritime trade in which one partner found all or most of the capital and the other traded in his own name. The societas on the other hand had its root in the more permanent association of the family or of persons who had full confidence in each other for the purpose of carrying on, in common, industrial and commercial enterprises in city or town. Both extended the scope of their application, commendas were formed for inland trade and partnerships of the collective type for maritime commerce. Each however developed on its own lines. In the commenda, where from the first the capitalist must have as a rule remained unknown to the merchants who traded with the active partner, the limited liability of the capitalist and the unlimited liability of the active partner were before long firmly established, while in the open " societas " the right of the individual partner to represent and bind the firm on the one hand, and on the other his unlimited liability for its debts, were finally recognised. Both types, modified in points of detail, have passed into modern commercial life. If the commenda has

[1] Endemann, *op. cit.*, pp. 395—6 and 55, 56.

developed into the "Société en commandite," the "societas" has its historical counterpart in the modern "Société en nom collectif" and the Offene Gesellschaft.

A third type of partnership, that of joint-stock companies with the capital in the shape of freely alienable shares, with a liability limited to the amount of capital represented by the share, and with an administrative governing body composed of shareholders in which the majority decided, was in process of formation during the Middle Ages.

To the origin of this type of partnership many causes contributed, but the decisive cause was the growth of colonial enterprises in Italy in the 15th century, and in Holland, France and England in the 16th and 17th centuries. A recent German writer[1] has attributed a great influence upon the birth and development of these companies to a peculiar form of partnership with limited liability that in shipping enterprises was common both in Northern and Southern Europe during the earlier part of the Middle Ages. At Amalfi, for example, in the 11th century the owners, the captain, and even the common sailors all had a share in the profits of the voyage and formed an association whose liability was strictly limited[2]. But it can hardly be said that the adoption of this peculiar form of partnership had a great influence upon the formation of joint-

[1] Lehmann, *Geschichtliche Entwickelung des Aktienrechts* (1895). *Das Recht der Aktienegesellschaften* (1898).

See Thaller, *La Société par Actions dans l'Ancienne France*, pp. 14, 15. Thaller, *Traité Élémentaire de Droit Commercial*, p. 163 note.

[2] Wagner, *Seerecht*, pp. 8, 9. Thaller, *Société par Action*, p. 15.

stock enterprises. No doubt it offered an example of a partnership with limited liability, but so did the far more common commenda; and the essence of a joint-stock company does not consist in the principle of limited responsibility, but rather in the prolongation of the corporate existence and organisation of the company beyond the life of its members and in the free negotiability of the shares.

Of greater influence were the public loans[1] raised by Italian cities during the 13th and following centuries. The loans were divided into shares (luoghi) and the names of the owners were registered in special books. The shares not only passed to the heirs in case of the owner's death, but could be freely bought and sold; and as negotiable shares, even though they cannot in any sense be regarded as shares in a commercial speculation, they showed the keen commercial mind of the Italian an expedient that might be adopted for raising capital for commercial as well as for military purposes. It was in Genoa that the first joint-stock companies arose. To cover the cost of the conquest of Chios and Phocaea (1346) a loan was raised by the Genoan state and as usual was divided into shares of 100 lires, and the shareholders were given the "dominium utile" of the conquered lands. This Colonial company, incorporated with the bank of St George in 1513, continued to exploit the resources of the two islands until their conquest by the Turks in the 16th century. Far more important however was the founding of the great bank of St George in 1407 when the various state

---

[1] Pertile, II. i. pp. 508—510. Goldschmidt, 292.

loans were consolidated into a single state debt. As security for the interest the city granted important privileges to the holders of the new consolidated stock, which was divided into shares of 100 lires. The stockholders were granted the right (1408) to carry on banking business, and especially after 1453 the administration and exploitation of important Genoan colonies passed into their hands. The creditors of the Genoan state had become the shareholders of a great colonial company which ultimately governed and administered Corsica, Kaffa and the greater part of the foreign dominions of Genoa[1].

Colonial expansion in England, France and Holland led, though much later, to the creation of companies similar to that of Genoa. The Compagnie des Iles d'Amerique, which seems to be the earliest example in France, was created in 1626 and was rapidly followed by others of the same type[2]. The Dutch East India Company (1602) was but little earlier. In England the East India Company[3] received a royal charter in the opening year of the 17th century. At first the company could hardly be considered as a joint-stock company; for in the early years of its history the voyages were separate and not necessarily permanent ventures of the sub-

[1] Pertile, II. i. p. 509.

[2] Viollet, op. cit., p. 767. Thaller, Société par Actions, p. 5, says "on ne doit pas remonter plus haut que le règne de Henri IV.": but he gives no example for this earlier date.

[3] Article on East India Company in Palgrave's Dictionary of Political Economy.

Levi, History of British Commerce, pp. 233, 337 and note.

scribers, who contributed varying amounts to the capital required for the expedition and received a proportionate share of the proceeds when the expedition returned. A shareholder in one of the early expeditions might or might not be a shareholder in the next. In 1613 the first so-called joint-stock was subscribed, but the term is misleading, it was not a subscription of permanent capital. As late as the middle of the 17th century subscribers wished to carry on separate trade in ships of their own, but the company protested and in 1654 a decision of the council of state was given "in favour of joint-stock management and exclusive trading."

It would seem that joint-stock companies took their rise owing to colonial expansion in Italy at the close of the Middle Ages, and had spread to Holland, France and England by the 17th century. The history of the development[1] and of the gradual extension of this form of partnership from projects of colonisation to commercial undertakings of every kind and variety lies outside the scope of this essay. But it is interesting to note that that system of partnership that now controls most of the great commercial and industrial enterprises of modern life, that has popularised and democratised capital and enabled the savings of the people as a whole to be applied to commercial speculations, great and small, of every kind, and that has changed the whole nature of commercial finance, was in its origin the outcome of state necessities and of colonial expansion.

[1] Especially interesting seems the combination of the commenda with the new form as seen in the *Commandite par actions*.

It is impossible in a short survey of the history and development of commercial law in medieval times to trace even briefly the history of every one of the manifold contracts of a mercantile character; but the history of insurance, owing to its intrinsic importance and to the fact that it took its present shape and form in medieval times and may be fairly regarded not as a creation of the legislature but of the merchants and traders themselves, would seem to claim especial reference.

As a special contract insurance dated only from the opening years of the 14th century. But long before that time an indirect secondary form of insurance was in common use in the trading countries of Europe. In sea loans, in contracts of commenda, for example, it is extremely common to find the risk made the object of a special clause, by which the contracting party who received the goods either expressly took over risks by land or sea, and became responsible for the safe delivery of the goods—salvi in terra—or expressly disclaimed all responsibility for the goods in case of misadventure.—Ad tuum resegum—ad risicum et fortunam Dei, maris et gentium—sana eunte nave—are the most usual forms of the clauses[1] by which the intention of the parties was declared. A passage in the oldest law treatise of the crusading kingdoms of the East, the "Livre des assises de la cour des bourgeois," shows that the use and legal signification of these clauses

[1] For these clauses see very numerous references and the treatment of the subject by Goldschmidt, p. 349 and following pages.

were well established as early as the 12th century.
"If it happen," declares the treatise[1], "that a man
entrust to another man his property to carry over
sea for gain 'en aventure de mer et des gens,' and
pirates happen to fall in with them and carry off all
that he is carrying, or the weather is bad and wrecks
the vessel and all is lost, reason commands that he
is quit in all, and that he need make no amends.
And if he has received the merchandise of good folk
to carry it 'sauf en terre,' he is bound by the law
and by the Assize to make amends according to
what he may have lost." Both clauses were in
common use, and merchants and capitalists began
to regulate the profit or commission according as
they assumed the risk or not. From a 14th century
(1335—1343) treatise on commerce, Pegolotti's
"Practica della Mercatura," it is evident that according as Florentine bills on England contained one
or other of these clauses the banker received a
commission of 10 "sous" per 100 marks or of only 20
"little sous[2]." Such differences in commission or in
share of profit were really premiums paid for the
risk undertaken, and it was but a natural result
that merchants began to make special contracts of

---

[1] *Le Livre des Assises des Bourgeois,* cap. 48, quoted in French
Translation of Bensa, p. 1. "S'il avient que un home baille à un
autre home de son aver à porter sur mer, à gaaing en aventure de
mer et des gens, et il avient que corsaus l'encontrent et li tolent
tout can que il porte, o il fait mauvais tens, et brise le vaisseau et
pert tout, la raison commande qu'il en est atant quite et il ne li en
deit riens amender. Et c'il avint que il resut l'aveir des bones
gens à porter sauf en terre, il est tenue de l'amender comment
qu'il seit puis perdus, par dreit et par l'asize."

[2] Bensa, *Il Contratto di Assicurazione,* pp. 31—2.

insurance. This there is every reason to believe they began to do in the opening years of the 14th century; for the earliest evidence goes back no further, and the absence of all reference to insurance in the vast mass of 13th century commercial documents of Marseilles and of the East makes it extremely probable that insurance had not developed into a special contract until the commencement of the 14th century. A clause in the statutes of the Calimala Gild of Florence of the year 1301[1] may or may not refer to special contracts of insurance, but that such contracts were in use in 1319 is proved by the books for that year of the great Florentine house of Del Beni. The entries in the books of this firm show that it paid to the Bardi, who acted as the forwarding agents of the firm, special sums for insurance[2]. For 1329 a receipt has been preserved in which the payment of 272 golden florins is acknowledged "in pagamento de risico et securitate facta per dictum dominum Gaspalem supradicto Nicolao Guicciardini pro supradictis mercantiis[3]." The documents show[4] that at this time the freight and insurance were contracted for simultaneously with the owners of the

---

[1] St. Calimalae (1801), Lb. ii. c. 4, p. 93. "Si vero aliqui mercatores euntes extra Florentiam vel morantes fecerint inter se pacta vel ordinamenta de aliquo rischio de avere quod portaverint, consules compellant tam ipsos viatores quam eorum sotios et magistros ea efficaciter observare." Quoted by Goldschmidt, p. 359, note 78.

[2] Bensa, *Il Contratto di Assicurazione*, pp. 51—53. Document i. p. 184.

[3] Bensa, *op. cit.*, p. 53.   [4] *Op. cit.*

ship in which the goods were to be conveyed.
Shippers were the first insurers. The earliest
contract of insurance which has been preserved
dates from the year 1347 and is interesting as
showing the care taken to avoid all suspicion of
usury. The insurer feigns to have received a loan
"gratis et amore" of the sum of money for which the
insurance was effected and promises faithfully to
return it, unless the ship arrives safe and sound
in port[1]. The contract of insurance had freed itself

---

[1] A.D. 1347. Brought to light by Bensa, Document iii. p. 192.
"In nomine D. Amen. Ego Georgius Lecavellum civis Janue
confiteor tibi Bartholomeo Basso filio Bartholomei me habuisse et
recepisse a te *mutuo gratis et amore* libras centum septem Janue.
Renuncians exceptioni dicte pecunie ex dicta causa non *habite*,
non *recepte*, non *numerate* et omni juri.

Quas libras centum septem Janue, vel totidem ejusdem monete
pro ipsis, convenio et promitto tibi solemni stipulationi reddere et
restituere tibi aut tuo certo nuntio per me vel meum nuncium.

Usque ad menses sex proxime venturos, *salvo et reservato, et
hoc sane intellecto, quod si cocha* tua de duabus copertis et uno
timono, vocata S. Clara que nunc est in portu Janue parata, Deo
dante, ire et navigare presentialiter ad Majorichas, *iverit et
navigaverit recto viagio* de portu Janue navigando usque ad
Majorichas et *ibi applicuerit sana et salva, quod tunc* et eo casu
sit praesens instrumentum cassum et *nullius valoris* ut si facta (sic)
non fuisset. Suscipiens in me omnem risicum et periculum dicte
quantitatis pecunie quousque dicta cocha applicuerit Majoricis,
navigante recto viagio ut supra. Et etiam si dicta cocha fuerit
sana et salva in aliqua parte, usque ad dictos sex menses, sit
similiter praesens instrumentum cassum et nullius valoris ac si
factum non fuisset. Et similiter si dicta cocha mutaverit
viagium sit dictum instrumentum cassum et nullius valoris ac si
factum non fuisset.

In dictum modum et sub dictis conditionibus promitto tibi
dictam solutionem facere, alioquin penam dupli dicte quantitatis
pecunie tibi stipulanti dare et solvere promitto cum restitutione

from its connection with the contract for the freight and had assumed the form of a feigned loan. For some 20 years it continues in the documents to retain this form, but from 1368 onwards it begins to take the guise of a feigned sale[1] "nomine venditionis

damnorum et expensarum que propterea fierent vel sustinerentur litis vel extra, ratis manentibus supradictis sub ypotheca et obligatione bonorum meorum, habitorum vel habendorum.

Actum Janue in Banchis in angulo domus Carli et Bonifaci Ususmaris fratrum, anno dom. nat. MCCCXXXXVII. indit. xv. secundum cursum Janue, die xxiii Octobris circa vesperas. Testes Nicolaus de Tacio draperius et Johannes de Rechio filius Bonanati cives Janue."

[1] Bensa, Document 8, p. 200. Contract of Reinsurance for July 12, 1370. "Nos Griffedus Benavia et Martinus Maruffus cives Janue confitemur tibi Bartholomeo Lomellino civi Janue q. Surleonis Nos a te *emisse*, habuisse et recepisse tot de tuis rebus et mercibus—Renunciantes......

... dare et solvere libras centum viginti quinque Janue hinc ad menses sex proxime venturos...

Salvo et specialiter reservato, si illa quantitas quarumcunque rerum et mercium, ad rixicum cujus Jullianus Grillus se obligavit Johanni Sacho sub certa reservatione, juxta formam publici instrumenti, scripti manu publici notarii, et que onerata fuit in cocha patronizata per Bartholeum Verme de Saulo, vel alium pro eo, in portu Clusarum de Flandria, sana et salva conducta et exornata fuerit, tunc et eo casu praesens instrumentum sit cassum et nullius valoris et pro rato.

Et risicum hujusmodi inceptum esse intelligatur quum dicta cocha in Cadese primo applicuit."

(In margine) : Eundo Clusas recto viagio, possit capere ubicunque. Non teneamur de aliquo tributo dato seu soluto in Cadese alicui.

Cf. Bensa, No. 9 and Contract of Insurance for 1425, Bensa, no. 16, p. 223 : "Confessi fuerunt sese emisse, habuisse et recepisse tot de ipsius Antonii rebus et mercibus causa infrascripta...salvo et specialiter reservato etc...." and no. 19 (1427 A.D.), p. 228.

et cambii." From the first it was required that the
person in whose favour the contract of insurance was
made should have a real interest in the safe arrival.
Insurance was not considered as a mere wager
dependent on the safe arrival of the ship, but was
a true contract of indemnity. For instance, in a
contract of insurance (1370) made on behalf of a
certain Rapallo, the insurer promised that Rapallo's
right should not be prejudiced by the fact that he
has no share in the ship, which implies that the
contract, without this special clause, might have
been invalidated by this circumstance. In course of
time however the clause—"habeat vel non habeat,
participet vel non participet" or more briefly, "habeat
vel non "—were introduced in the contracts of insurance, and finally this clause was always included.
It is not probable however that this clause made it
a matter of indifference ·whether the insured had a
real interest in the safe arrival of the ship or not,
for very often it was stated that, while the insured
had no interest in the particular goods insured, he
contracted the insurance to safeguard other interests :—"protestans quod in praedictis non participat,
sed haec fieri facit pro sua electione, cautela, cautione,
et juvimento[1]." The two clauses would seem to

---

[1] Bensa, p. 66. "Non è però a credere che questa clausola
importasse esenzione assoluta dell' assicurato da ogni necessità
d' interesse al salvo arrivo della nave, ma piuttosto che fosse
diretta a ribadire il concetto che qualunque sorte d' interesse
potesse legittimamente coprirsi colla difesa dell' assicurazione. Se
così non fosse, non avrebbe spiegazione la clausola, bene spesso
apposto nei contratti. 'Protestans quod in praedictis non par-

show that an interest of some kind was necessary
and that an insurance which was a mere wager was
not allowable. In the early documents ship or goods
alone or ship and goods together were objects of insurance. When it was goods that were insured, the
ship in which they were to be transported was clearly
indicated. Insurances of goods to be conveyed in an
unnamed ship—in quovis—were rare even in fairly
late times, but even as early as the middle of the
14th century there was a special case in which the
ship was left uncertain. When goods had to be
transhipped at an intermediate port, the choice of
the fresh ship was sometimes at least left to the
insured[1]. In the Genoan documents the limits of the
time within which the insurer was responsible for
the risk were carefully fixed. In the case of the
cargo the risk began from the moment the ship set
sail, and was terminated when the goods were

---

ticipat, sed haec fieri facit pro sua electione, cautela, cautione, et
jhuvimento." Goldschmidt, pp. 370—1, note 114, opposes this
view. "Vielmehr wollen sie (*i.e.* the clauses) augenscheinlich dem
Versicherten den Nachweis des Interesses überhaupt ersparen;
ja sie lassen die Deutung zu, dass sogar den Nachweis des mangeln-
den Interesses ausgeschlossen sei." Legislation however, Goldschmidt adds, soon declared against such contracts. "Jedenfalls
ist die Gesetzgebung bald dagegen eingeschritten, sei es, dass
dergleichen Verträge nur mit Erlaubnis der Regierung gestattet
wurden ; sei es, schlechthin untersagt."

[1] Bensa, p. 66, and document 6, p. 197 (1350 A.D.). For an
insurance "in quovis" with no ship specified, see Bensa, No. 24,
p. 236 "...Super illa navi patronizata per *quamvis* personam quam
ascendet et veniet dictus Nicolaus Andreas Cibo..." A.D. 1488.

Bensa, p. 70, refers to Straccha who discusses this clause and
who declares that it was common in English policies.

disembarked[1] in port. For the ship, on the other hand, the insurance held good until the ship had reached its port of destination safe and sound and had remained there 24 hours[2]. That property already lost at the time of the contract of insurance, but the loss of which was unknown at the time, could be legally insured is shown by the fact that in contracts where the insurance was effected not for a definite voyage but, as was occasionally the case, for a definite time, which however did not usually amount to more than a year, the risk was sometimes declared to run before the date of the contract. Change of route from the first freed the insurers from all risk. The clauses in the early documents, borrowed from

---

[1] V. Bensa, p. 70, *e.g.* Insurance of Merchandise in ship to sail from Aigues-Mortes to Ephesus and Rhodes. Bensa, Document 13, p. 216. "Salvo et specialiter reservato, si illa quantitas rerum bonorum et mercium...*conducta* et EXONERATA fuerit *in ipsis locis* Teologi et Roddi, vel altero eorum, ad salvamentum, *tunc* et eo casu praesens instrumentum sit cassum etc....et intelligatur inceptum hujusmodi rixicum, cum dicta navis recesserit et velificaverit de Aquis mortuis, et stet et duret, eundo, stando, navigando, onerando, et exonerando patronus, de dicto loco Aquarum mortuarum usque ad dicta loca Teologi et Roddi, quomodocumque et qualitercunque voluerit, quousque dicta quantitas rerum, bonorum et mercium *conducta* et EXONERATA fuerit in Teologo et Roddo, vel in altero ipsorum duorum locorum ad salvamentum." No. 14, p. 218; insurance on goods from Montrone to Aigues-Mortes. "E quando la detta roba sarà *posta* e SCARICA in terra a salvamento in Aqua Morta che in quello caso i detti assicuratori siano liberi e disobbligati della sicurtà per loro fatta."

[2] v. Bensa, p. 70, and Document, p. 213. Insurance of a galley, 1394. "Salvo et specialiter reservato, si quedam galeacia" etc...."applicuerit in dicto portu Janue ad salvamentum et ibi steterit per xxiiii horas, *tunc* et eo casu" etc. Also no. 16 (A.D. 1425), p. 223.

the contracts of sea loan—recto viagio, eundo et
redeundo, recto et continuato viagio—were short
and strict, but by the end of the 14th century a
·clause had been elaborated which is substantially
the same as that in use in modern times and which,
while allowing all reasonable freedom of action,
insists that the destination shall not be changed :—
"eundo, stando, navigando, onerando, exonerando
patronus a dextris et a sinistris, per rectum et
indirectum, antecedendo retrocedendo, quocunque
ubicunque, quomodocumque et qualitercumque
voluerit patronus vel alius pro eo, *viagio tamen non
mutato*[1]." The "consilia" of the jurist Bosco (1399—
1435) show that by common usage the insurers were
not held responsible for losses caused by barratry on
the part of the captain. "I confess," he writes,
"that by the common and unwritten custom of the
country, and by the general and tacit understanding
of those concluding the contracts, there is one
exceptional case in which the risk pertains to the
insured, to wit when it is proved that the things
were lost of set purpose by the fraud and contrivance
of the captain[2]."

The Genoan contracts do not specify in detail the
dangers against which the insurance is effected, and
Bosco argued that the insurance applied to all
misadventures " usual or unusual." In Pisan and

---

[1] Bensa, p. 71, who refers to Straccha's 17th century treatise
on insurance. The clause is found almost verbatim in an
insurance upon a ship for the year 1425. Bensa, no. 16, p. 224.

[2] Bensa, 74, and for Bosco, French Translation of Bensa,
p. 29, note 2.

Florentine contracts, on the other hand, the enumeration is so complete and detailed as to leave little loop-hole for evasion on the part of the insurers. The risks which the insurers run, declares a Florentine contract of insurance for the year 1397, are " of God, the sea, of nations, fire, jettisons, restrain by Lords or by communes or any other person, of letter of marque, of arrest and of every other case, peril, fortune, impediment or mishap which in any way could occur or might have occurred, no matter how or under what condition the cases might occur, excepted only what concerns custom dues and ballast[1]." It was not unusual in the contract for insurers especially to except certain risks for which they did not wish to be held liable, and general average was often thus excepted by a not uncommon clause : " non teneantur de devastato corpore navis ad salvamentum tunc existentis[2]." The premium was paid in advance, and this was almost inevitable in the earlier stages of the contract when insurance assumed the form of a feigned sale. With such a form of contract the insurer would have no legal remedy against his debtor for the premium. Later on the custom of prepayment of the premium was in several places enforced by the law.

---

[1] Bensa, Document 14, pp. 217—8. A.D. 1397. "E il rischio che gli assicuratori corrono in sulla detta roba... ; si è di Dio, di mare, di gente, di fuoco, di gitto di mare, di ritinemento di signori o di comuni, o d' alcun altra persona, o di rappresaglie o d' arresto e d' ogni altro caso, pericolo, fortuna, impedimento o caso sinistro, che per verun modo ne potese intervenire o fusse intervenuto, e fussono fatti i casi come si volessero o di che condizione, salvo di stiva o di dugana."   [2] Bensa, p. 76.

Originating in the early years of the 14th century as a separate contract, insurance developed rapidly and by the close of the century was, in Italy at any rate, a common form of contract. In 1393 a single Genoan notary within 3 weeks drew up no less than 80 contracts of insurance[1], and the consilia of Bosco (1399–1435) which have in recent times been rediscovered by Bensa bear out this view and declare that a contract insurance was " no unusual thing," but " such as many merchants of Genoa make, of whom some have no other mode of livelihood than this[2]." The law and customs of insurance are in their main outlines the outcome of the usage of merchants as expressed in the written contracts of insurance.

The clauses of these contracts by the 15th century had broadly speaking taken the form and substance that for centuries and even in modern times they were to retain. Legislation was to declare and sometimes to modify the law, and judicial decisions were to recognise fresh usages as they gradually arose, and to give precision and a fixed signification to the clauses that substantially unaltered were repeated from century to century in contracts of insurance, but the clauses of the early contracts remain the basis of the modern law of insurance of the civilised

[1] Bensa, p. 79.

[2] Bensa, p. 79, quotes Bosco: "Marcus propter lucrari fecit plures assecurationes sicut faciunt plurimi mercatores de Janua quorum aliqui de nullo alio vivunt quam de hujusmodi quaestu, qui quandoque est utilissimus, quandoque damnosus, secundum cursum temporum et fortunae blandimenta vel adversiones. Unde Marcus non facit rem insolitam sed rem usitatam et consuetam fieri in Bancis a plurimis, etiam ex sapientioribus."

world. Policies of marine insurance are to this day
made in a form which on the face of it is clumsy,
imperfect, and obscure. But the effect of every
clause and almost every word has been settled by a
series of decisions, and the common form really implies a whole body of judicial rules, " which originated
either in decisions of the courts upon the construc-
tion or on the mode of applying the policy, or in
customs proved before the court so clearly or so often
as to have been long recognised by the courts without further proof. Since those decisions and the
recognition of those customs, merchants and under-
writers have for many years continued to enter into
policies in the same form. According to ordinary
principle, then, the later policies must be held to
have been entered into upon the basis of those
decisions and customs. If so, the rules determined
by those decisions are part of the contract[1]." Upon
the framework of the old contract of insurance
elaborated in Italy during the closing centuries of
the Middle Ages and transferred by international
trade to the other commercial countries of Europe, a
vast and complex body of Law has been reared. To
a certain extent it is new wine in old bottles. The
modern law of insurance is more complicated and far
more precise than the law and custom of the 14th or
15th centuries, but the development from the old to
the new has been slow and natural, and the old and
the new alike have the same underlying general
principles. The development of the legal rules and

---

[1] 3 Q. B. Div. 558, 562, quoted by Pollock, *Contracts*, pp.
258—9.

principles of insurance has in reality been effected
by the natural development in the usages of the
merchant class, and judicial decisions and legislation
have everywhere done little but recognise and enforce
those usages and check those particular forms of
insurance that were liable to grave abuse. Thus the
early laws of Genoa and Barcelona forbid insurances
to the full value of the cargo. A Genoan law passed
about 1420 only allowed insurances to the amount of
half the value of the ship including the value of the
equipment, though an earlier statute had permitted
insurance of two-thirds of the value[1]. In Barcelona
the regulations of 1435 only allowed insurances on
goods in native ships to be effected to three-fourths
of the value and declared that any excess of this
amount should not be recoverable by the insured,
though the insurers were entitled to retain the full
premium paid: if loaded on board foreign ships
however the goods could only be insured to the
extent of half their value[2]. Modified in 1436 and
1458 this rule received (1484) the form that it long
retained. in the important regulations of Barcelona
on insurance, which were translated into various
languages and exercised a considerable influence
upon the law of insurance by giving precision to the

[1] Bensa, Document vi. p. 159. "Participibus vero vasorum et
navigiorum liceat assecurari se facere usque ad medietatem
valoris et pretii, vel estimationis dictorum vasorum et navigiorum,
computato etiam armamento ipsorum": for earlier statute, Bensa,
p. 89, and note 1.

[2] Pardessus, *Collection des Lois Maritimes*, vol. v. pp. 496—7;
Regulations of 1435, c. 3. For case of foreign ships, cap. 4, pp.
495—6.

usages and promoting uniformity in the laws of the chief countries of Europe. "The councillors and prudhommes ordain," declares the first chapter of these regulations, "that all ships and other vessels of our Lord the King, and those of foreigners of whatever nation they may be,......and all goods loaded and transported by them to any part of the world, to whomever it may belong whether subjects of our Lord the King or foreigners, may be insured at Barcelona, to wit those of the subjects of our Lord the King for seven-eighths, and those of strangers for three quarters of the real price which the things insured shall have cost, in which price shall be reckoned the expenses of- the expeditions, the cost of the insurances, and other expenses[1]."

In Italy the earliest regulations absolutely forbade all insurances in favour of foreigners, but a more enlightened policy prevailed and the restrictions fell into desuetude, and during the course of the 15th century full liberty of insurance was conceded at Genoa to foreigners except for voyages between the various ports of the Mediterranean and of the Black Sea. In Barcelona the various regulations issued during the same period mark an advance in the same direction. The earliest law of 1435 did not allow the insurance of foreign goods in foreign vessels, while the regulations of 1484 simply limit the amount of the insurance.

In both Italy and Barcelona legislation during the 15th century declared contracts of insurance invalid when the loss of the property insured was

---

[1] Pardessus, *op. cit.*, vol. v. p. 524.

known or might reasonably be supposed to be known at the time the contract was signed[1], and the Barcelona statute of 1484 "to remove all incertitude as to the time when the news may have been known" allowed for every league that the news had to travel by land an hour from the time that the news first reached dry land. The early Spanish and Italian legislation also settled the question of jurisdiction in cases relating to insurance, and both alike conferred it upon the commercial courts[2]. On the whole however the early legislation did but regulate existing usage, and the immediate origin of the principles of insurance lies in customs and contracts of the medieval merchants of Italy.

[1] Bensa, for Italy, p. 89. For Barcelona, Pardessus, v. p. 514 (St. 1458, cap. 14), pp. 536—7 (St. 1484, cap. 17). For other city regulations see Goldschmidt, p. 379, n. 137.

[2] Bensa, Document 3, p. 153. "De his autem praemissis cautionibus et securationibus que fierent inter cives seu districtuales Florentie et pro mercantiis et rebus eorum vel alicujus eorum, possit et debeat per *dictum officium* (*i.e.* of the Mercanzia) cognosci procedi, jus fieri et terminari...et tales securationes... debeant observari et executioni mandari simpliciter et secundum bonam fidem et *consuetudinem mercatorum*." Pardessus, v. p. 513, note 1; p. 512, St. 1458, cap. 9. "Aucun assuré ne pourra decliner la competence ou juridiction de la dite cour du consulat, ni porter des affaires ailleurs qu'a ladite cour."

CONCLUSION.

THE whole history of Law Merchant in Europe during the Middle Ages was characterised by a constant advance towards uniformity and by the successful assertion of new principles of law. It was developed in local courts, in which directly or indirectly the merchants declared the law. The merchants of the fair courts of St Ives, or the merchants and mariners of Barcelona, were alike the "doomsmen" of the court; it was the function of the judge merely to proclaim and execute the judgment of the merchants. In Italy the judges occupied a more important position; but here again they were wholly or in part taken from among the merchants, as was the case in the later commercial courts of France and Germany. The international nature of trade even in medieval times, the general similarity in economic conditions that gradually arose, and the predominant influence of the legal conceptions and the commercial usages of the Italian merchants, all combined to make the law administered by merchants to merchants more uniform and international in character. It is however difficult to draw a hard and fast line separating the Early Law Merchant from the Modern. All dividing lines in the history of human institutions are to a certain extent arbitrary and artificial. Still in the 16th century the Law Merchant entered upon a new stage of its development, and its early history may fairly be regarded as closed. All the great principles that mark the commercial law of modern times had then been evolved and successfully asserted, and different forces and influences were becoming important in determining its future history and development. The age of the great writers on mercantile law, of Marquardus, Straccha and Malynes, was dawning. Legislation, not so much of single cities, as in the earlier period, but of great and powerful kingdoms with definite commercial policies of their own, began freely to declare and to modify the law. The period of formation when the Law Merchant had to indicate important principles opposed to the principles alike of Roman and Germanic law was passed, and the early history of the law, the history of the creation and successful assertion of its leading maxims in the local courts of fair or town or staple, ended, as so much of medieval history ended, in the 16th century. By that time every great country in Europe had recognised in commercial cases the principles of representation, the negotiability of bills of exchange, the liability of the real property of the debtor for his debts, the validity, to a certain extent at least, of formless contracts, the necessity of speedy justice, the importance of the principles of equity and the claims of the bona fide possessor to the protection of the law. The legal

relations of partners to one another and to the outside
world had, in almost every important point, been
definitely settled, and a new commercial contract,
insurance, had been evolved and the legal principles
that were to govern its development clearly marked.
The medieval merchant had laboured, and the
modern world had entered into his labours.

Both Canon and Roman law exercised an influence
upon the development of the Law Merchant. Canon
law recognised the principle of representation[1], laid
stress upon equity and good faith and on the binding
force of a simple promise, and exerted a favourable
influence on the growth of summary methods of
procedure. So far its influence was on the side of
the Law Merchant. On the other hand the prohibition of usury by the Church cramped and hindered
trade, and so far as it was effective simply served to
raise the rate of interest. But the importance of the
laws against usury has often been greatly exaggerated.
When necessary, the merchant rarely failed to find
expedients to evade them and did not hesitate upon
occasion to defy them. At Genoa, for example, any
attempt to make use of the Canon law on usury in
order to invalidate contracts of insurance was strictly
forbidden and punished. Moreover the Church itself
gradually relaxed the rigour of the law; the canonists
began to recognise the right of the lender to compensation for "damnum emergens" and "lucrum
cessans" and "the total result was that any merchant
or indeed any person in a trading centre where there

---

[1] C. 68, 72, de reg. juris, in vi. (5.12), referred to by Goldschmidt, p. 276, note 139.

were opportunities of business investments (outside money lending itself), could with a perfectly clear conscience and without fear of molestation contract to receive periodical interest from a person to whom he lent money ; provided only that he first lent it to him gratuitously for a period which might be made very short, so that technically the payment would not be reward for the use, but compensation for non-return of the money[1]." On the whole the doctrines and principles of the Canon law told in favour of the Law Merchant. On several important principles the two systems of law were in substantial and permanent agreement, while the prohibition of usury by the Church was not difficult to evade and, as opportunities for the employment of capital increased with the general expansion of trade, that prohibition was gradually relaxed.

Roman law had a vastly greater influence than Canon law upon the Law Merchant in Western Europe. Numerous rules of Roman law found their way into the great Sea Code of Barcelona ; and in spite of bitter complaints the English Admiralty continued to make use of the "Law Civil." At Como and Pera, Piacenza and Cremona, Bologna and Florence the special mercantile statutes expressly refer to the Roman law as a subsidiary source to be used where the statutes gave no rule[2]. The vast mass of early commercial documents of the lands of the Mediterranean and the fair bonds of the

---

[1] W. Ashley, *Economic History*, vol. i. part ii. p. 402.

[2] Lattes, *Il Diritto Commerciale nelle città Italiane*, p. 72, and p. 76, note 11.

Netherlands are drawn up in the technical language of the Roman lawyer. It is true that perhaps the most striking feature of these early commercial contracts is the almost invariable renunciation by the contracting parties of many of the "exceptions" and rules of Roman law; but this very renunciation would seem to imply that in the absence of express renunciation the principles of Roman law were applicable.

Roman law was, in the main, the basis of commercial contracts and consequently, in the main, the basis of the Law Merchant. "It is a most notable fact, but not on that account less important," writes Lattes in a work in which the mercantile statutes of the medieval cities of Italy have been examined and analysed with scrupulous care and thoroughness, "that in the theory of obligations, the Roman laws, preserving an authority much greater than in any other part of the law, were applied, transcribed and imitated, so as to form the basis of modern codes, with the few modifications imposed in recent times. To the modifications the mercantile statutes contributed much....*But these statutes themselves...in reality only contain a few fragmentary dispositions and a few remarkable exceptions to the principles of Roman law*[1]." "The contract of affreightment, the doctrine of general average, and the contract of bottomry" are all covered by the principles of Roman law[2].

---

[1] Lattes, *op. cit.* p. 122.

[2] Carter, *English Legal Institutions*, p. 268. Cf. Goldschmidt, 78, and note 93.

But great as was the influence of Roman law, the customs and usages of the merchant himself remained the decisive factor in the development of the Law Merchant. When the true interests of commerce were at stake the merchant persistently and obstinately refused to recognise the rules of Roman law. The principle of representation was carried in the Law Merchant far further than ever Roman law carried it; the honest purchaser was protected, and formless contract recognised, to a large extent, as binding. The Law Merchant no doubt rested upon a solid basis of Roman law, and in later times as commerce with the discovery of the new world and the growth of capital became more world-wide and approximated more closely to the commercial relations of the vast Roman Empire, direct borrowing from Roman law became perhaps more open and more extensive. Even in England Lord Holt and Lord Mansfield introduced whole branches of the civil law[1]. But in medieval times the merchant in the long run rejected or accepted, extended or restricted, the principles of the Roman law as the interests of commerce required. In no small measure Roman law was the raw material of the Law Merchant, but that material the medieval merchant fashioned and framed as seemed good to him. "Out of his own needs and his own views" the merchant of the Middle Ages created the Law Merchant.

[1] Smith, *Commercial Law*, Historical Introduction.

APPENDIX I.

Willelmus de Temesford queritur de Augustino
Capello de Temesford, quod Idem Augustinus iniuste ei
detinet et non solvit III. quarteria frumenti, que de eo
mutuavit die Jovis proxima post Invencionem Sancte
Crucis anno regni regis Edwardi XVI°., et unum quarterium siliginis et unum quarterium brasii que similiter
eidem Augustino tradidit per particulas prout indiguit:
precium tocius bladi XXXII. solidorum. Quod quidem bla-
dum debuit ei solvisse ad festum Sancti Michaelis proxi-
mum sequens, unde Idem A. nichil hactenus ei persolvit,
set totum detinuit et adhuc detinet ad dampnum suum.
Predictus Augustinus presens dicit se non fuisse at-
tachiatum per quod attachiamentum respondere debuit,
et consideratum fuit quod respondisset ad incopamentum
dicti Willelmi: qui quidem Augustinus respondere
noluit, set in contemptu tocius Curie recessit. Quare
considerandum fuit, quod dictus Willelmus a prefato
Augustino tanquam de indefenso recuperaret debitum
suum unacum dampnis suis, et quod predictus Augustinus pro iniusta detentione fuisset in misericordia,
plegius i equs. Et super hoc venit quidem Walterus
Daneys et optulit se probaturum dictum equm esse suum
et ad hoc petiit admitti cum probacione sua, cui
responsum fuit ex parte adversa, quod fraudulenter
optulit se probaturum alienum catallum. Et quia idem
Walterus in calumpnia sua tenebatur pro suspecto eo
quod inhonesta persona fuit nec habuit tantum in

catallis et quod ipse per fraudem et collusionem hoc
fecerat, consideratum fuit quod inde rei veritas per
bonam inquisicionem inquireretur, utrum dictus equs
erat suus tempore attachiamenti vel non. Et super hoc
electa fuit inquisicio. Que venit et dicit per sacramentum suum quod dictus Walterus Daneys equm
predictum arravit per argentum Dei de prefato Augustino in villa de Temesford die dominica proxima ante
attachiamentum factum ; quod quidem attachiamentum
suum erat die Martis sequenti, set in decepcione dicti
Willelmi de Temesford et per collusionem, ut idem
Willelmus elongaretur de catallis suis ; et ponitur in
respectum judicium donec per mercatores melius dis-
cuciatur. Et convocatis mercatoribus de diversis
communitatibus et aliis in plena Curia, consideratum
est quod dictus Walterus Daneys, ex quo nunquam
posuit se in Inquisicione predicta que quidem Inquisicio
capta erat adtunc tanquam ex officio senescalli et ex quo
Idem W. per argentum dei collatum prefato Augustino
empcionem equi predicti secundum legem mercatoriam
sufficienter confirmavit, quod idem Walterus veniat cum
tercia manu sua de bonis hominibus electis et fide dignis
ad probandum dictum equm esse suum, ita quod dictus
Augustinus tempore attachiamenti in eodem equo artem
habuit neque partem. Qui quidem Walterus venit et
sufficienter fecit legem. Ideo idem W. inde quietus cum
equo predicto et prefatus Willelmus pro falso clamore in
misericordia et condonatur.

APPENDIX II.

Curia de Mercurii proxima post festum sancti Dunstani Nicholaus Legge queritur de Nicholao de Myldenhal quod iniuste eum impedit quod partem habere non potest de quodam bove quem Nicholaus de Myldenhal emerat in presencia sua in villa sancti Ivonis die lune ultimo preterito secundum usum Mercatorum ad dampnum suum duorum solidorum, desicut promptus erat solvere medietatem peccunie cuius tota summa continebat viis. vid.

Et predictus Nicholaus defendit verba Curie et dicit quod lex mercatorum bene permittit quod quilibet Mercator participet de mercandisa carnificum si partem inde in tempore vendicionis calumpniaverit, set quod ipse Nicholaus Legge non fuit presens tempore empcionis nec partem calumpniavit promptus est facere quod Curia considerat. Et Nicholaus Legge dicit quod prefatus Nicholaus de Mildenale ad legem venire non debet eo quod incopatus fuit quod debuit ei negasse habere partem bovis predicti, quod quidem verbum non defendebat. Quare Idem N. Legge petit judicium de ipso sicut de indefenso. Unde consideratum est quod dictus N. Legge recuperet versus ipsum is. pro dampnis suis. Et Idem N. de Mildenale in misericordia iis.; plegius Johannes de Thoref.

APPENDIX III.

Willelmus de Pappeworth queritur de Johanne de
Kent quod idem Johannes iniuste ei detinet viginti tres
solidos et quatuor denarios de uno equo vendito eidem
Johanni pro xliii*s*. iv*d*. et pro uno quadrante ei
tradito ad argentum dei die Mercurii proximo preterito
in Curia Willelmi Manger apud sanctum Ivonem ; quos
quidem denarios idem Johannes debuit solvisse incon-
tinenti eidem : de quibus non solvit nisi tantum xxiii*s*.
iv*d*. et totum residuum scil. xx*s*. retinuit et adhuc
detinet ad dampnum ipsius Willelmi dimidium Marce et
ducit sectam.

Et predictus Johannes presens defendit verba que
fuerant defendenda et dicit expresse se in nichillo ei
teneri et quod ita sit promptus est ad verificandum per
Legem suam si Curia consideraverit.

Et predictus Willelmus dicit quod ad legem venire
non debet racione quod incopavit ipsum Johannem fuisse
seysitum de i quadranti eidem tradito nomine argenti
Dei quod quidem argentum Dei idem Johannes non
defendit et insuper petit iudicium et consideracionem
mercatorum si predictus Johannes per legem suam
adnichilare possit accionem et demandam ipsius Willelmi

necve. Et ponitur judicium in respectum propter tenuitatem curîe usque diem Mercurii. Ad quem diem consideratum fuit per Mercatores quod, ex quo contractus factus inter dictum W. querentem et prefatum J. defendentem affirmatus fuit per quadrantem datum predicto Willelmo in argentum Dei, quod quidem argentum Dei dictus J. non defendebat, remaneret tanquam indefensus. Et dictus W. reciperet etc. et Johannes in misericordia II *s.* Solvit, et taxata sunt dampna ad II *s.*

APPENDIX IV.

Vitalis de Grafham conquerens optulit se per Robertum de Grafham attornatum suum versus Hugonem Pope super iniusta detentione. Et testatur quod dictus Hugo districtus fuit per unum equm, qui est in Curia Abbatis, die lune proxima post festum sancti Dunstani ultimo. Et super hoc venit quidam Alanus de Berkhamsted die martis proxima sequenti et allegavit in plena Curia dictum equm esse suum et quod ipse illum equm emerat ad opus suum proprium de quodam Thoma de Rammesden, et quod ita sit voluntate sua spontanea posuit se in Inquisicione et pars adversa similiter. Et inquisicio scilicet Ricardus Scot Radulphus Scot Adam faber Absalom Sterne Johannes de Waltham Walterus …veniunt et dicunt per sacramentum quod dictus Alanus iniuste calumpniat equm predictum tanquam suum nec habet partem in eodem quia Idem Alanus ad opus predicti Hugonis eundem equm emit tanquam valettus et abrokator eiusdem Hugonis et quod idem Hugo mandavit ei…London quod solueret nomine eiusdem Hugonis viginti solidos pro eodem equo; quos quidem denarios idem Alanus mutuo recepit predicto die lune de Radulpho de Honcton de sancto Ivone; et hoc ex recognicione dicti Radulphi. Quare consideratum est quod predictus equs teneatur et capiatur plus donec dictus Hugo justificaverit se ad respondendum predicto Vitali vel suo attornato et apreciatus est equs per Willelmum de Hocton Nicholaum Legge Thomam de…et Johannem Pake Juratos ad ii Marcas. Et datus dies predicto atornato usque in crastinum apostolorum Philippi et Jacobi in proximis Nundinis futuris.

APPENDIX V.

Alicia uxor Nicholai le Tanur queritur de Matilda Ffraunceys; plegii de prosequendo Nicholaus Tannator et Mauritius Sutor; plegii defendentes vir eius et Hugo Bacun. Et partes optulerunt se et Alicia dicit se nolle prosequi versus prefatam Matildam super tres busselos brasii inventos in manibus predicte Matilde pro quibus ipsa ad querelam dicte Alicie fuit attachiata. Ideo ipsa Alicia et plegii sui scilicet Nicholaus le Tanur et Mauritius Sutor pro non secta sua adiudicata est ad Carcerem et de Carcere fecit finem per xiid.

Et super hoc senescallus ex officio suo tanquam pro secta domini Regis petiit a dicta Matilda Ffraunceys in cuius seysina dictum brasium fuit inventum qualiter se defendere voluerit quod brasium predictum furtive non fuerat perquisitum. Que dicit quod de bono et malo ponit se in Deo et in vicinis juratis; qui veniunt et dicunt per sacramentum suum quod quidam extraneus de quo ipsa Matilda non habuit noticiam dictum brasium portavit ad domum ipsius Matilde; super quod brasium ipsa Matilda ad instantiam dicti extranei tradidit ei ex mutuo VIII denarios nec habuit ipsum extraneum suspectum de aliquo latrocinio. Et ideo consideratum est quod dicta Matilda eat inde quieta unacum brasio suo predicto.

AUTHORITIES.

Black Book of Admiralty, ed. Travers Twiss, 1871—1876.

Britton, ed. Nichols, 1865.

Bracton, *Tractatus de Legibus*, 1569.

Little Red Book of Bristol, ed. Bickley, 1900.

Munimenta Gildhallae, ed. Riley, 1859—1862.

Records of Leicester, ed. Bateson, 1899.

Records of St Ives' Fair for the year 1275, ed. F. W. Maitland in *Select Pleas in Manorial Courts*.

Records of St Ives' Fair for the year 1291. (Augmentation Office Court Rolls, Portf. 16, No. 16.) A few cases are given in the appendices.

Select Pleas of the Court of Admiralty, ed. Marsden, 1892 —1897.

Statutes of the Realm, vol. i. 1810.

Bergamo, *Gild Statutes of* 1457, ed. 1780.

Brescia, *Gild Statutes of* 1429, ed. 1788.

Florence, Statutes (1301) *of Calimala Gild*, ed. Filippi, 1889.

Genoa, *Leges Genuenses*, ed. Poggi, 1901.

Mantua, *Gild Statutes of* 1400, ed. Portioli, 1887.

Pisa, *Statuti de Pisa*, ed. Bonaini, 1859—1870.

Monumenta Historiae Patriae, especially the two volumes: Chartae, Leges Municipales.

Monumenta Historico-juridica Slavorum Meridionalium.

Deutsche Rechtsquellen des Mittelalters, ed. Wasserschleben.

Hildesheim Urkundenbuch, vol. i.

Urkunden zur städtischen Verfassungsgeschichte, ed. Keutgen, 1901.

Documents relatifs à l Histoire de l'Industrie et du Commerce en France, ed. Fagniez, 1898—1900.

Documents inédits sur le commerce de Marseille au Moyen Age, ed. Blancard, 1884, 1885.

Collection de Lois Maritimes, ed. Pardessus.

Arias, *I Trattati Commerciali della Repubblica Fiorentina*, 1901.

Arias, *Studi e Documenti di Storia di Diritto.*

Bensa, *Il Contratto di Assicurazione nel Medio Evo*, 1884.

Bensa, *Histoire du Contrat d'Assurance au Moyen Age*, traduit par Valéry, 1897. This translation does not contain the documents of the Italian original.

Bonolis, *La Giurisdizione della Mercanzia in Firenze nel Secolo XIV*, 1901.

Brunner, *Deutsche Rechtsgeschichte*, vol. ii. 1892.

Brunner, *Forschungen*, 1894.

Bruschettini, *Trattato dei Titoli al Portatore*, 1898.

Carter, *English Legal Institutions*, 1902.

Cunningham, *Growth of English Industry and Commerce*, vol. i. 1896.

Del Vecchio e Casanova, *Le Rappresaglie nei Comuni Medievali*, 1894.

Desjardins, *Introduction historique à l'Étude du droit commercial maritime*, 1890.

Des Marez, *La Lettre de Foire à Ypres*, 1901.

Doren, *Untersuchungen zur Geschichte der Kaufmannsgilden des Mittelalters*, 1893.

Endemann, *Studien in der romanisch-kanonistischen Wirthschafts- und Rechtslehre*, 1874.

Freundt, *Das Wechselrecht der Postglossatoren*, 1899.

Glasson, *Les Juges et Consuls des Marchands*, 1897.

Goldschmidt, *Handbuch des Handelsrechts*, vol. i. 1891.

Goldschmidt, *Vermischte Schriften*, 1901.

Gross, *Gild Merchant*, 1890.

Hegel, *Städte und Gilden der germanischen Völker*, 1891.

Heusler, *Deutsches Privatrecht.*

Holdsworth, *History of English Law*, 1903.

Holtzendorff, *Encyklopädie der Rechtswissenschaft*, 1904.

Huvelin, *Le Droit des Marchés et des Foires*, 1897.
Huvelin, *Travaux Récents sur l'histoire de la Lettre de Change*, 1901.
Huvelin, *L'Histoire du Droit Commercial* (Conception Générale, État Actuel des Études), 1904. An exceedingly useful Bibliography.
Jenks, *Early History of Negotiable Instruments*, in *Law Quarterly Review*, vol. ix.
Lastig, *Entwickelungswege des Handelsrechts*, 1877.
Lattes, *Il Diritto Commerciale nella Legislazione Statuaria delle Città Italiane*, 1884.
Lattes, *Studii di Diritto Statuario*.
Morel, *Les Juridictions Commerciales au Moyen Age*, 1897.
Pertile, *Storia del Diritto Italiano*, 1896—1903.
Pollock and Maitland, *History of English Law*, 1898.
Pollock, *Principles of Contract*, 1902.
Rezzara, *Dei Mediatori e del Contratto di Mediazione*, 1903.
Scrutton, *Elements of Commercial Law*, 1891.
Silberschmidt, *Die Entstehung des Deutschen Handelsgerichts*, 1894.
Smith, *Mercantile Law*, 1890.
Sohm, *Die Entstehung des deutschen Städtewesens*, 1900.
Stevens, *Commercial Law*, 1903.
Thaller, *Traité Élémentaire de Droit Commercial*, 1900.
Thaller, *Les Sociétés par Actions dans l'Ancienne France*.
Viollet, *Histoire du Droit Civil Français*, 1893.
Wagner, *Seerecht*, 1884.

INDEX.

CAMBRIDGE: PRINTED BY J. AND C. F. CLAY, AT THE UNIVERSITY PRESS.